the **Chief**

Santa Fe
the Indian-detour

The
Atchison, Topeka & Santa Fe
Railway System
Time Tables

Corrected to August 15, 1934.

NOVEMBER, 1963 — APRIL, 1964

**Burlington
Route**

SYSTEM
TIME TABLE

Way of the Zephyrs
AND VISTA-DOMES

**ILLINOIS
CENTRAL**

PANAMA LIMITED ALL-PULLMAN STREAMLINER
Chicago • St. Louis • New Orleans
CITY OF NEW ORLEANS ALL-COACH STREAMLINER
Chicago • St. Louis • New Orleans
CITY OF MIAMI PULLMAN AND COACH STREAMLINER
Chicago • St. Louis • Florida
GREEN DIAMOND PARLOR CAR AND COACH STREAMLINER
Chicago • Springfield • St. Louis
LAND O'CORN ALL-COACH STREAMLINER
Chicago • Dubuque • Waterloo

ISSUED JANUARY 25, 1953

**PENNSYLVANIA
RAILROAD**

FORM 1

ISSUED OCTOBER 26, 1

ALTIMORE
HIO RAILR

ME TABLES

NDENSED
TRAIN
HEDULES
EAST
and
WEST

NDARD TIME

B&O

Route of the Dieseliner

CLASSIC
AMERICAN RAILROADS

Mike Schafer

Motorbooks International
Publishers & Wholesalers ®

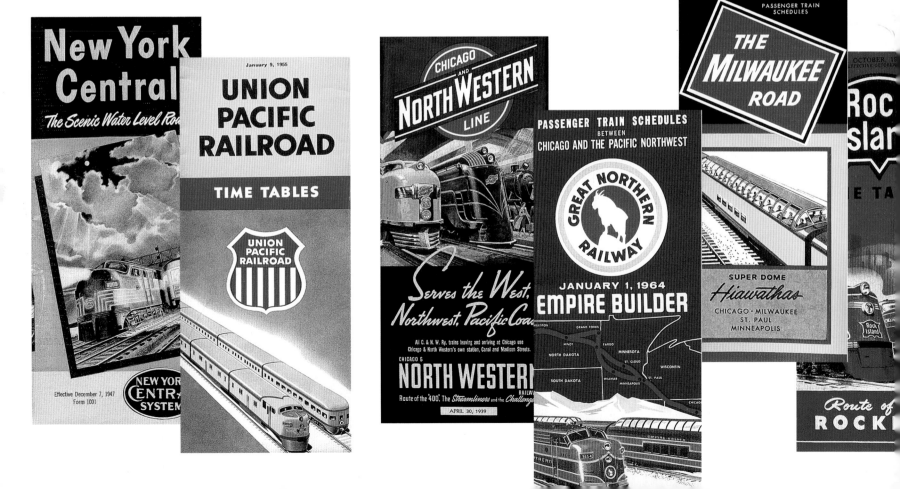

Acknowledgments

I confess. I didn't do this book all by myself. If I had, I'd probably still be working on it, and you'd be reading some other book.

No, a book like this requires enlisting the varied skills of many people, and I'm fortunate to have a number of friends and contacts who don't mind my calling them at all hours to ask questions or ask for help. (At least, they didn't *say* they minded.)

First of all, I would like to thank Jim Mischke who authored most of the Baltimore & Ohio and Union Pacific chapters and proofread several others for historical accuracy. Through Jim, I was also able to come up with some fine photo material.

Instrumental in documenting various facts throughout the entire book was Mike Blaszak. As an attorney in the railroad industry, Mike was my first choice for proofreading, checking and double-checking facts, and interpreting the sometimes convoluted nature of railroad history. In addition, Mike authored much of the Chicago, Rock Island & Pacific chapter, the "Rock" being one of his pet railroads.

The fact that the Pennsylvania Railroad is Dan Cupper's pet road resulted in my drafting him to proof the PRR chapter. As much as I like the Pennsy and have explored much of its territory, only Dan could figure out some of the unknown photo locations through my describing the photos to him over the phone.

In a similar vein, many thanks must go to Robert Willoughby Jones of Pine Tree Press for his assistance with the Boston & Maine chapter. As an accomplished editor and the author of a beautiful book on the B&M, Robert was my first choice for assisting me with the chapter on that New England favorite for CLASSIC AMERICAN RAILROADS.

Questions about the Santa Fe? I always direct those to Joe McMillan, of McMillan Publications, known for its line of fine Santa Fe books. Joe also served for many years as an employee of the Atchison, Topeka & Santa Fe, so his help with the Santa Fe chapter was especially welcome.

As for questions about New York Central—a railroad I've long been intrigued by but don't know that much about—I rely upon (and give thanks to) C. W. Newton. I'm certain Chuck knows more about the Water Level Route than anyone I know, and his collection of NYC resource material continues to amaze me.

This is primarily a photo book, so the help I received from numerous photo contributors was immeasurable. Hundreds of wonderful photos were submitted, and narrowing them down to the final 200 or so necessary for this book's format was often an agonizing task. Their names, of course, appear with their respective photos. In particular I must thank my longtime friend Jim Boyd, editor of *Railfan & Railroad* magazine. Jim and I have known one another for over 30 years, during which both of us have traveled extensively—oftentimes together—on various railroad photography expeditions. As a source for post 1950s U.S. railroad photography, Jim is second to none in terms of quality and scope.

I would be remiss if I also didn't thank Bill Caloroso, Steve Glischinski, Bob Penisi, and my friends and associates within my own company (Andover Junction Publications), Joyce Mooney and Steve Esposito.

In closing, I would also like to thank the good folks at Motorbooks International, my mom for having me, my sister for putting up with me when we were kids, and my dog Max. Did I forget anybody? I hope not. I'm going to need more help on my next book.

Mike Schafer

First published in 1996 by Motorbooks International Publishers & Wholesalers, 729 Prospect Avenue, PO Box 1, Osceola, WI 54020-0001 USA

© Andover Junction Publications, 1996.

Maps within reprinted with permission from K-3 Directory Corporation.

Book design and layout by Andover Junction Publications, Andover, New Jersey, and Waukesha, Wisconsin

Library of Congress Cataloging-in-Publication Date Available
ISBN 0-7603-0239-1

On the front cover: Clad in Santa Fe's revered "warbonnet" paint scheme, designed in 1937, new General Electric diesels race through Chalender, Arizona, with a westbound intermodal train on September 18, 1995. The Atchison, Topeka & Santa Fe Railway was arguably the best-known railroad in the world. From the late 1800s to September 22, 1995, when the railroad merged with Burlington Northern, Santa Fe's web of steel linked the Midwest with Texas and the Great American West. *Howard Ande photo*

On the frontispiece: Electro-Motive passenger locomotives of Western giants Southern Pacific, Union Pacific, and Santa Fe form a classic lineup at Los Angeles. *Jim Boyd photo*

On the title page: Union Pacific's great *City* Streamliner fleet was once an esteemed network of transcontinental trains linking the Midwest with the West Coast. Today, UP's goodwill train, used for business and excursion service, utilizes the historic equipment from those great trains as it rovers about the vast UP system. Here it reposes at St. Louis in 1993. *Dan Munson photo*

On the back cover: Blanketing the Northeast and Midwest and connecting nearly all major cities therein—New York, Chicago, Pittsburgh, St. Louis, Detroit—the great Pennsylvania Railroad was almost a country unto itself. On August 21, 1955, locomotive 460 hustles through Tuckahoe Junction, New Jersey, with the Ocean City branch train. The locomotive today resides in the Railroad Museum of Pennsylvania. *John Dziobko photo*

Printed in Hong Kong

Contents

Santa Fe presented one of the most familiar faces in U.S. railroading.—DAN MUNSON.

Foreword

For over 100 years beginning with their introduction to North America in the 1830s, railroads played a dominant role in American life. Whether it was helping to tame the wild frontier, moving the goods of a growing nation to market, or taking Auntie Em to visit her relatives, railroads touched almost every facet of American life. At one time nearly everyone had a relative who worked for a railroad, or knew someone who did.

Over time, several railroad companies came to dominate the American scene. Companies like the mighty Pennsylvania Railroad, the "Standard Railroad of the World." Or the Atchison, Topeka & Santa Fe, which became celebrated in the song of the same name. Railroads were even tied to American history: The Chesapeake & Ohio called itself "George Washington's Railroad" since a predecessor company was chartered by the first President; sister Baltimore & Ohio—featured in this book—was the nation's first railroad. Northern Pacific's charter was signed by Abraham Lincoln, while rival Great Northern was founded by James J. Hill, surely one of the most famous and colorful of the nation's "railroad magnates" of the 19th Century.

Today these railroads are fondly called "classics." In this volume, author Mike Schafer has assembled a photographic tribute to several of these colorful companies. Mike is uniquely qualified to tell the stories of America's classic railroads. He grew up in Rockford, Illinois, at the doorstep of Chicago, America's Railroad Capital. A talented writer and photographer, Mike has traveled throughout North American to capture enduring images of railroading. He often rode the rails on these journeys, traveling aboard such classic trains as Milwaukee Road's *Hiawatha*s, Union Pacific's *City of Los Angeles*, and the famed *Broadway Limited*, late of the Pennsylvania Railroad.

Most of the classic railroads recalled here have now vanished, absorbed into the huge "mega-systems" that today comprise the majority of America's rail network. Thanks to the photographers whose work is presented here, those classics live again in the pages of CLASSIC AMERICAN RAILROADS.

Steve Glischinski
Shoreview, Minnesota
April 1996

Introduction

What was the trickiest part of assembling this book? No doubt about it: choosing the railroads! After all, what constitutes a "classic" railroad? There are no hard and fast definitions of what makes a railroad "classic." In fact, it's all pretty subjective. If I had asked a dozen of my railroad cohorts to list 15 classic railroads—while trying to maintain some semblance of geographic balance—I'm certain no two lists would have been the same.

Oh, there are certain lines no one would dare leave out of a first volume about classic railroads: Santa Fe, Pennsylvania, Southern Pacific and New York Central are perennial favorites. But how about the rest? For every additional railroad I included, I had to leave out two runners-up. But then, that leaves plenty of potential candidates for possible future volumes, doesn't it?

For this volume, I based my selections on a railroad's longevity, public recognition, accomplishments, and location.

Longevity: I arbitrarily required a railroad to have existed for at least a half century. It takes time for a railroad to "age" into a classic. After all, you don't stomp your feet in the grapes on Monday and expect to drink the wine from those grapes on Friday . . . even if your feet *were* clean.

Public recognition: I selected railroads that, at least within the region they served, enjoyed at least a modicum of recognition by the general public.

Accomplishments: I included railroads I felt had made notable contributions to the railroad industry as well as to customers. For those railroads who seemed to be perennially down on their luck (the Rock Island immediately comes to mind) and were struggling merely to survive much less make "notable contributions," I included them anyway, for their charm if nothing else.

Location: I wanted every region of the U.S. represented by at least one railroad that the region could call "its own." This was a little problematic for the Southeast, where traditionally good photo coverage remains sparse, but Louisville & Nashville aficionados came through with some nice material.

The histories have been written to provide an overview and are not meant to be comprehensive. Likewise, photo selection was aimed at exuding the flavor of each railroad and is not meant to be a complete documentation of the railroad at hand. Indeed, every one of the railroads in this book warrants a book of its own.

While you are reading this book and savoring the photos, note how the various railroads were inextricably interlinked, even when they were rivals. Notice, too, how closely all were tied to the lands and the people. No doubt about it. Railroads have long been part of the fabric of life in America, and many have become icons that are as classic as '57 Chevys and reruns of "Leave it to Beaver."

Mike Schafer
Waukesha, Wisconsin
May 1996

FACING PAGE. Railroads had many time-honored traditions, and that of a conductor—the boss of the train—conferring with his engineer prior to departure was just one of them. At Louisville, Kentucky, on a humid, cloudy day late in the summer of 1971, a Louisville & Nashville conductor and engineer compare trip itineraries prior to highballing for Nashville with the Florida-bound *South Wind.*—MIKE SCHAFER.

Atchison, Topeka & Santa Fe

It may well be the best-known railroad in the world. It had its own movie and popular song. It operated one of the most renowned passenger trains in the world (the *Super Chief*). Its striking red-and-silver "warbonnet" diesel paint scheme—one of the most well-recognized corporate images ever designed—adorned nearly every boy's electric train set. And, its identity was nearly inseparable from that of the American Southwest, a region long steeped in lore, adventure and mystique. More importantly, perhaps, is that the Santa Fe had always enjoyed a reputation of providing high-quality freight and passenger service.

The infant Santa Fe—first known as the Atchison & Topeka Railroad, chartered in 1860—had a relatively modest goal: to connect the Kansas cities of Atchison and Topeka with Santa Fe, New Mexico. This it did, although construction did not begin until 1868, five years after President Abraham Lincoln signed legislation providing land grants to the railroad.

Renamed Atchison, Topeka & Santa Fe in 1863, the railroad built westward through southern Colorado and Raton Pass (vying with the Denver & Rio Grande Railroad for exclusive occupancy of the pass; Rio Grande lost the battle) thereby tapping coal mines and livestock production. Not only did the abuilding railroad reach Santa Fe, but also it built right on to Albuquerque, New Mexico, in 1880. Ironically, the city of Santa Fe ended up being served by what became a branch off the Kansas City-Albuquerque main route.

Once Santa Fe and Albuquerque had been reached, it was only natural for the railroad to target California—in part at the behest of that state, which was in the throes of being monopolized by the Central Pacific (Southern Pacific). Construction crews struck west from Albuquerque, reaching the state line at Needles, California, in 1883. From there, Santa Fe used a line built by Southern Pacific to Barstow, California, which it later acquired. At Barstow, the Santa Fe met the California Southern Railroad, which had built north from San Diego in 1885. Los Angeles was reached in 1887. Construction of the San Francisco & San Joaquin Valley Railroad together with the acquisition of trackage rights over SP's Tehachapi Pass brought the Santa Fe to the San Francisco Bay area in 1900.

The second half of the 1800's saw unprecedented railway construction throughout the U.S., and Santa Fe was in the thick of it. By the end of the century, Santa Fe had reached Denver (1882) and Chicago (1888) and down into Texas from Kansas including a line to the Gulf of Mexico at Galveston.

The expansion continued into the 20th Century, notably with the 1908 completion of the Belen Cutoff between Belen and Texico, New Mexico. Connected to an already existing route that came down off the Kansas City-Colorado main through Amarillo, Texas, the Belen Cutoff became the crucial final link for an efficient east-west route which would avoid the steep grades of Raton Pass. This pathway thus became the main freight route for Chicago-California freight traffic, while the original route over Raton continued to be used by most Chicago-California passenger trains.

The completion of a through route between the Belen Cutoff and Coleman, Texas, in 1914 provided a short cut for traffic moving between the Gulf of Mexico and the West Coast. Throughout much of this mainline construction period, Santa Fe had also blanketed Kansas and Oklahoma with branch lines and had gained control of various smaller, subsidiary railroads that further strengthened the company's network. In terms of size, Santa Fe reached its zenith in 1931 with 13,568 route-miles and for many years enjoyed the status of being the longest railroad in the U.S.

The Santa Fe was arguably America's most-famous railroad—and certainly one of the most successful. Freight and passengers rode over Santa Fe rails from the late 1860s until 1995 when the AT&SF merged with Burlington Northern to form the Burlington Northern Santa Fe Railroad. FACING PAGE: Four new General Motors diesels wind through Sullivans Curve in California's Cajon Pass with a Los Angeles-bound intermodal train during the spring of 1992.—SCOTT HARTLEY. FACING PAGE INSET: Santa Fe's celebrated red, silver, black and yellow "warbonnet" paint scheme, designed in 1937 by 43-year-old Leland Knickerbocker of General Motors' Industrial Design Department for the new, streamlined *Super Chief*, became a hallmark of the Santa Fe. Not only did the design and colors continue to be used on some new locomotives delivered in 1996 to the newly merged BNSF, but they appeared on thousands of toy and model trains manufactured during the 60 years the timeless scheme has endured.—BRIAN SOLOMON. LEFT: A timetable from 1934 featured artwork of the Grand Canyon.

A brutish Santa Fe 4-8-4 (four pilot wheels, eight driving wheels, four trailing wheels) Northern-type steam locomotive marches toward the summit of Cajon Pass in California's San Bernardino Mountains with the third section of train No. 24, the eastbound *Grand Canyon*. This was a popular Los Angeles-Chicago train geared for tourists destined to its namesake. Although Santa Fe's Chicago-California main line bypassed the Grand Canyon by some 60 miles, the railroad had a branch extending from the main line at Williams, Arizona, right to the rim of the canyon over which it operated connecting trains. Once at the canyon end of the branch, travelers could stay at Santa Fe's El Tovar Hotel, managed by Santa Fe affiliate Fred Harvey Corporation.—WILLIAM D. MIDDLETON.

With extremities that linked Gulf ports, Pacific Coast ports and the inland port—and railroad hub—of Chicago, Santa Fe was strategically positioned to become one of the strongest rail carriers in North America—which it did. Not only did the railroad serve as a distribution system for imports and exports moving through its gateway cities, but it provided steel arteries for food products and manufactured goods produced on U.S. soil.

For all its extensive successes as a freight carrier, the Santa Fe was perhaps best remembered for its fleet of stylish passenger trains, several of which lasted until 1971. The railroad's panache for passenger treatment harkened to the 1892 inauguration of the *California Limited* as the premier train on the road's Chicago-Los Angeles route. This was followed by the 1911 debut of the extra-fare *De Luxe* between Chicago and L.A. Then, on November 14, 1926, a legend was born: the *Chief*, another extra-fare Chicago-Los Angeles

train. Ten years later, on May 12, 1936, the railroad one-upped itself with the introduction of the all-sleeping-car *Super Chief*, yet another entry in the Chicago-L.A. market—and the first to be non-steam-powered, being pulled by a pair of primitive, boxy diesel locomotives built by General Motors-owned Electro-Motive Corporation (EMC). A year later, the *Super Chief* received all new equipment, emerging as Santa Fe's first lightweight streamliner. Its new streamlined EMC diesels debuted what was destined to become one of the most-famous railroad paint schemes in the world, the red, silver, black and yellow "warbonnet" livery. For the next 40-plus years, these colors would appear on all locomotives regularly assigned to Santa Fe passenger trains. (Santa Fe freight diesels also wore an Indian-motif livery, but in various combinations of blue and yellow.) In 1938, the all-coach streamliner *El Capitan* was launched as the *Super Chief*'s companion train (the two ran only a

SANTA FE AT A GLANCE

Headquarters: Chicago, Illinois

Mileage:

1950: 13,074 including subsidiary roads
1995 (prior to merger with Burlington Northern): 9,126

Locomotives owned as of 1963:

Diesel: 1,855

Rolling stock owned as of 1963:

Freight cars: 84,439   Passenger: 1,235

Principal routes as of 1950:

Chicago-Los Angeles via Kansas City, Mo., and La Junta, Colo.
Emporia, Kan.-Galveston, Texas via Oklahoma City, Okla., Fort
  Worth and Houston, Texas
Emporia, Kan.-Dalies, N.M.
Barstow-Richmond, Calif.
Temple-Farwell, Texas
Denver-La Junta, Colo.
Albuquerque, N.M.-El Paso, Texas
Dallas-Presidio, Texas
Kansas City-Tulsa

Principal passenger trains

Super Chief (Chicago-Los Angeles)
El Capitan (Chicago-Los Angeles)
The *Chief* (Chicago-Los Angeles)
Grand Canyon (Chicago-Los Angeles)
The *Scout* (Chicago-Los Angeles)
San Francisco Chief (Chicago-San Francisco, Calif.)
Texas Chief (Chicago-Houston)
San Diegan (Los Angeles-San Diego)
Tulsan (Kansas City-Tulsa)
Chicagoan (Dallas-Kansas City-Chicago)
Golden Gate (Los Angeles-San Francisco)

ABOVE: Classic Santa Fe Electro-Motive (General Motors) F7-type diesels pose at the California State Railroad Museum, Sacramento, in 1992.—ALEX MAYES. BELOW: System map from 1967 Santa Fe passenger timetable.

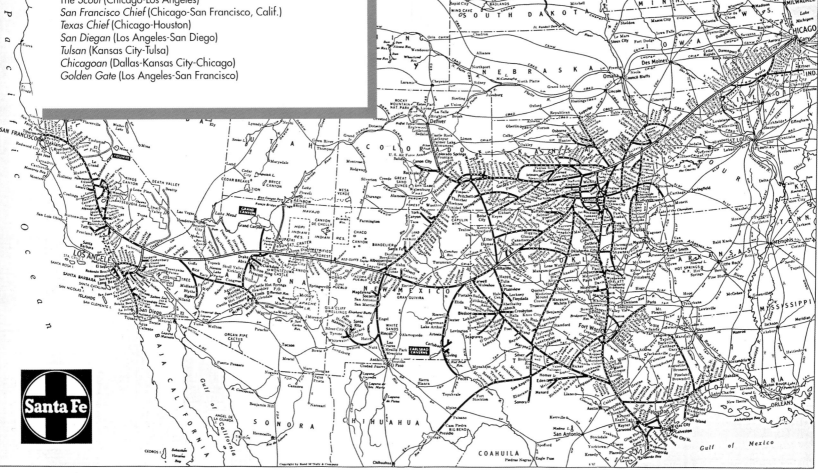

few minutes apart), serving economy travelers who wanted a fast trip over the main line.

Still more *Chief*s joined the fleet, including the *Texas Chief* (Chicago-Fort Worth-Houston) in 1948 and *San Francisco Chief* (Chicago-Kansas City-Amarillo-San Francisco) in 1954. During this period, the *Super Chief* again was upgraded, in 1951, and now sported new sleeping cars, diner and its famous Pleasure Dome lounge. The Pleasure Dome car featured a smartly appointed lounge on its main level, while the upstairs dome section contained a raft of individual, fully rotating seats for unparalleled viewing. Unique to the Pleasure Dome car was the Turquoise Room dining area beneath the dome section—a private dining room that could be reserved for groups and served from the adjacent diner's kitchen.

Through consistent service and periodic upgrading and innovation (the Santa Fe was the first U.S. railroad to apply the bilevel concept to intercity rail travel with its 1956 introduction of "Hi-Level" passenger cars on the *El Capitan*), Santa Fe gained a reputation of operating the finest passenger trains in North America—a reputation held until Amtrak assumed operation of selected Santa Fe passenger trains on May 1, 1971. And throughout its history, Santa Fe's *Super Chief* was often cited as the world's best and most-famous passenger train, often hosting Hollywood stars and business titans.

Innovation and improvement on the AT&SF didn't pivot entirely on passenger trains, of course. The railroad was a pioneer in dieselization, acquiring its first freight diesels in 1935 at a time when most U.S. railroads pooh-poohed what was still an unproven method of moving tonnage over the main line. By 1941, Santa Fe was taking delivery of 80 new road freight diesel sets from Electro-Motive, which allowed the railroad to dieselize its desert territory, where water for steam locomotive operation was at a premium.

Santa Fe was also among the first to embrace the trailer-on-flat car—TOFC or "piggyback"—concept, in 1952, and it also experimented in air-freight service—under the name Santa Fe Skyway—in 1946. Federal regulations eventually put the kibosh on the latter, but piggyback and eventually other intermodal-type operations became a hallmark of the Santa Fe. For example, AT&SF can be

In replacing the steam locomotive, Santa Fe initially concentrated its dieselization program in desert territory where water was at a premium, and particularly in mountainous territory where extra locomotives were necessary to assist trains up the grades. TOP: In this 1950 scene, a quartet of new Electro-Motive diesels labor at moving a 70-car eastbound freight up Cajon Pass. The going-away view (ABOVE) of the same train shows a set of similar, but older, Electro-Motive diesels on the rear (for safety reasons, located ahead of the caboose) serving as "helpers" to lift the train over the summit of the mountains. Once over the hill, the helpers will be removed from the train and sent back down to San Bernardino, California, where they are based, to await the next train needing assistance.—BOTH PHOTOS, WILLIAM D. MIDDLETON.

LEFT: Only minutes into its 2,222-mile journey to California, the *Super Chief* glides away from the Chicago skyline on a summer evening in 1968. At a combined 7200 hp., the two new Electro-Motive FP45-model locomotives powering tonight's train should have no trouble keeping the *Super* on time across America. About ten minutes behind the *Super* will be its all-coach companion train, the *El Capitan*.—MIKE SCHAFER. BELOW: Aboard the *Super Chief*'s dining car, patrons could sample such fares as Tournedos of Beef or Santa Fe French Toast.—ANDY HUGHES.

credited for implementing, in 1963, the first top-lift crane for unloading piggyback trailers, and in 1976 it built the experimental "Six-Pack" six-unit "spine" car for carrying freight containers, which later became the standard design for intermodal equipment. Santa Fe and the St. Louis-San Francisco Railway (Frisco) also pioneered, in 1960, the concept of carrying automobiles on racks attached to flatcars (versus in special boxcars). Now, 70

percent of motor vehicle production goes to market this way.

"Fast" was a term most apropos for Santa Fe. Not only was AT&SF the shortest route between Chicago and southern California, but it was the fastest—for freight as well as passenger. The *Super Chief* cruised for long stretches at 90 mph to cover the 2,224 miles separating Chicago and L.A. in less than 40 hours including station stops. In 1968, Santa

Fe introduced the *Super C*, a high-speed limited-stop priority freight train that, on an experimental run, made the Chicago-L.A. trip in a record of 34 hours and 35 minutes.

Although American railroads in general were in turmoil during the late 1960s and throughout most of the 1970s, Santa Fe continued to be a strong force in the industry, refusing to succumb to the security of status quo. Having reluctantly shed its longtime commitment to what by 1971 had become an unprofitable endeavor—passenger trains—the railroad focused on its assets as a leading freight carrier. In pursuing new directions, Santa Fe took some unexpected turns. For example, Santa Fe participated in the construction of several new lines in Arizona and New Mexico to tap coal mines and electric generating stations.

In 1983, the road announced merger plans with one-time rival Southern Pacific, although the union was nixed by the Interstate Commerce Commission in 1986. In 1984, Santa Fe expanded through purchase of central Illinois shortline Toledo, Peoria & Western. In the late 1980s and 1990s, the railroad also reduced mileage considerably through sale or abandonment of numerous branch lines in the Midwest and South Central U.S. By the mid 1980s, Santa Fe was well under way in an important transformation: that of becoming the nation's leading intermodal carrier.

It's a fine, warm day in June 1973, and the photographer is hoping that the rattlesnake population stays hidden as he records a freight sweeping through the New Mexico high country near Mountaineer. Four blue-and-yellow diesels of GE and GM heritage lead the eastbounder along what was Santa Fe's main freight route between the Midwest and West Coast.—MIKE SCHAFER.

LEFT: Heart of the Santa Fe system was Argentine Yard and its locomotive shop complex at Kansas City, Kansas. During a spring evening in 1990, two General Electric diesels stand in the drizzle outside the main shop building. The locomotive at left appears to have just been sent out the door from its shop appointment, while the locomotive at right—completely shut down and with engine-access doors flung open—looks to be headed indoors for a serious going-over. BELOW: Inside the shop where it's warm and dry, two locomotives are being returned to tip-top performance by able Argentine shop forces.—BOTH PHOTOS, DAN MUNSON.

LEFT: Not all Santa Fe passenger trains were glitz and glamour. The shiny new diesels in this view from June 1954 just outside Los Angeles Union Passenger Terminal may suggest "*Chief*", but they're arriving with a train that is largely mail and express. Until the 1960s, U.S. railroads moved a significant amount of express and U.S. mail. Some of it was moved aboard mail and express cars handled by regular passenger trains, but if there was enough of the traffic, the railroads often scheduled a separate mail and express train.—WILLIAM D. MIDDLETON.

ABOVE: Appropriately named, the burgh of Matfield Green, Kansas, and its surrounding topography provide a verdant backdrop for train No. 195 cruising for California on a splendid June afternoon in 1986. The moribund stock pens harken to an era when nearly all livestock moved by rail to major market centers. The decentralization of the livestock industry after World War II brought an end to the once-familiar sight (and aroma) of strings of open-slat stock cars loaded with restless pigs and cattle.—SCOTT MUSKOPF. RIGHT: Four PA-type passenger diesels of the American Locomotive Company (Alco) ease a "Green Fruit Express" reefer train into Joliet, Illinois, on a rainy spring Saturday evening in 1965. Although the GFE nomenclature had formally been dropped by this time, it was still used by railroad crews in reference to any special movement of perishables in solid trains of refrigerator cars. For a time, surplus passenger locomotives occasionally were used to power such high-priority trains.—JIM BOYD.

Between 1985 and 1995, Santa Fe carried more loaded intermodal units (truck trailers and containers) than any other U.S. railroad. Underscoring its commitment to quality freight service on its principal routes, Santa Fe ordered hundreds of new diesel locomotives from General Motors and General Electric in the 1980s and 1990s.

In 1989, Santa Fe management made a surprise move that paid tribute to the railroad's esteemed past: For the first time in more than 20 years, the cherished red-and-silver paint scheme, which earlier had been reserved primarily for Santa Fe passenger diesels and had not been applied to new locomotives since 1968, would henceforth be applied to all new road-freight diesels being built for the railroad.

Though AT&SF-SP merger plans had been thwarted in the mid-1980s, a surprise 1994 announcement of merger with giant Burlington Northern ended with success. On September 22, 1995, the holding companies of BN and Santa Fe united, forming the largest (as of that time) railroad network in U.S. history: Burlington Northern Santa Fe. Thus closed the history books on one of the most-celebrated railroads to serve America.

Even the mighty Santa Fe is dwarfed in this dramatic scene near Mesta, Arizona. The date is January 20, 1994, and "double-stack" container trains such as this westbounder are the rule, not the exception, for most east-west freight traffic between the Midwest, Texas and California.—BRIAN SOLOMON.

For little Lariat, Texas, the towering grain elevator complex is the biggest show in town. Dwarfed by those elevators, two diesels clad in Santa Fe's somewhat short-lived "yellowbonnet" paint scheme switch grain hoppers on May 1, 1973. Lariat, some 20 miles southeast of the important Santa Fe division point of Clovis, New Mexico, was on the railroad's subsidiary Panhandle & Santa Fe, built to connect Sweetwater in central Texas with Santa Fe's primary east-west freight route at Farwell, Texas.—JOE MCMILLAN.

RIGHT: We're in Kingman Canyon, Arizona, as an east-bound freight rips across a dry wash in a scene that seems to have been pulled right out of an Arizona travel guide. It's September 17, 1995, and in five more days Santa Fe will merge with Burlington Northern, closing the book on what many say was the world's most-famous railroad.—HOWARD ANDE. BELOW: Fog and chilly drizzle shroud Joliet (Illinois) Union Station in an air of mystique during the holiday season of 1964-65 as train No. 12, the *Chicagoan*, makes its final station stop before closing in on the end of its run at Chicago's Dearborn Station, 38 miles and less than an hour distant. Number 12 originated in Dallas the previous day.—RON LUNDSTROM.

LINKING 13 GREAT STATES WITH AMERICA

Baltimore & Ohio

The United States' first common-carrier railroad, the Baltimore & Ohio, was born of desperation. Early 19th Century Baltimore merchants faced ruin. Their port competitors for inland trade were sponsoring vast public projects. Philadelphia was behind a transportation route to Pittsburgh comprised of canals and inclined planes, while the State of New York had its Erie Canal, extending all the way from the Port of Albany to Buffalo.

Baltimore's competitive edge was that it lay well inland on a well-protected harbor on Chesapeake Bay accessible to the National Road, but if merchants in New York and Philadelphia succeeded in lowering their transportation costs in the lucrative trade between the Atlantic Seaboard and the expanding American western frontier, Baltimore would wither as a worthy seaport.

Canals were only the truly proven transportation technology of the period, and Baltimore considered the feasibility of hooking up with the proposed Chesapeake & Ohio Canal in the Potomac River valley some 50 miles west of Baltimore. But those 50 miles were rugged and not conducive to canal construction. Baltimore made a bold alternative decision to thwart the competition: build one of them newfangled railroads. Thus, in 1827, the Baltimore & Ohio was chartered to link Baltimore to the Ohio River, well over 300 miles to the west. Construction began on the Fourth of July the following year.

Standing in the way were the ridges of the Allegheny Mountains and numerous other hills and rivers. With little technological base to draw upon, the railroad builders learned as they went. Some early decisions proved wrong, such as excessively winding the track route to provide easier grades. The early trains were able to tolerate heavy grades, but they inflicted excessive wear on the curves. Some mistakes would be corrected, financed with the growing revenue stream as the rail-

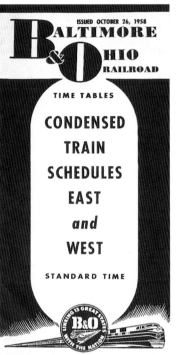

road expanded (segments opened for service as they were completed). Others would never be fixed, affecting the B&O's competitive position throughout its existence. B&O's grades in the Alleghenies, for example, would always be more challenging than that of rival Pennsylvania Railroad, requiring expensive extra power to move tonnage over the mountains.

Political barriers lay ahead as well. Conflicts with the C&O Canal for right-of-way along the Potomac River hampered construction for years. The Pennsylvania legislature, dominated by Philadelphia interests, prevented access to Pittsburgh and easier Allegheny Mountain crossings within Pennsylvania. Construction proceeded slowly, the main line reaching Cumberland, Maryland, in 1842 and finally the Ohio River at Wheeling, Virginia (West Virginia after 1863) in 1852. By this time, a branch had opened (in 1835) between Baltimore and Washington.

The B&O didn't stop at the Ohio River. It struck west from Grafton, West Virginia, on the Baltimore-Wheeling main line, and plugged through Ohio to Cincinnati and then across Indiana, and Illinois to Illinoistown (now East St. Louis, Illinois) by 1857, thus establishing rail service to the Mississippi River.

The outbreak of the Civil War placed the B&O squarely between the combatants as an asset to be exploited by each side and denied the other. Siding with the Union forces did not spare the B&O from periodic destruction and service interruptions for months at a time. Still, the logistical heroics of moving men and material vast distances over the B&O proved the worth of railroads to military operations.

After the Civil War, John W. Garrett, B&O president from 1858 to 1884, did much to expand the B&O. The railroad extended northwest into Ohio from Wheeling through the lease of two smaller roads which in 1869 brought it Sandusky, Ohio, on the shores of Lake Erie. A subsidiary finally opened a line

FACING PAGE: The Baltimore & Ohio was already over 125 years old when this evening view of early diesels in action was recorded in August 1956 at Eckhart Junction, Maryland, near Cumberland. The two locomotives—FA and FB models from the American Locomotive Company (Alco)—are heading west out of Cumberland and are about to dig into the B&O main line's climb out of the Potomac River valley known as Sand Patch Grade.—RODNEY PETERSON. **FACING PAGE INSET:** B&O always did things with an understated style and elegance, as is evident in this headstone over the doors of the railroad's division headquarters building at Grafton, West Virginia.—BRIAN SOLOMON. **LEFT:** A B&O passenger timetable from 1958.

For decades, the *Capitol Limited* was the flagship of the B&O, linking Chicago with the nation's capital. On a summer morning in 1966, the "*Cap*" has just backed into Chicago's Grand Central Station, concluding its overnight run from Washington, D.C. The train is extra long because of an ongoing nationwide airline strike that crippled travel during the summer of 1966. Hallmarked by its clocktower (at right in distance), the vintage depot, which sat just south of Chicago's Loop, opened in 1890 and eventually was purchased by the B&O. It was closed in 1969 and razed shortly thereafter.—MIKE SCHAFER.

from Cumberland to Pittsburgh in 1871, and the B&O reached westward to Chicago in 1874. Two great bridges were built across the Ohio River at Benwood (Wheeling) and Parkersburg, West Virginia, replacing slow and inefficient ferry operations. Yet on several vital fronts, Garrett was painfully outmaneuvered, especially by the Pennsylvania Railroad. First, Pennsy management discovered a latent charter to build a railroad from Baltimore to Washington, D.C., and did so in 1872, ending B&O's local monopoly. Then PRR acquired B&O's friendly eastern connection, the Philadelphia, Wilmington & Baltimore in 1881 and terminated important traffic arrange-

ments to Philadelphia and New York. B&O was forced to build its own line to Philadelphia, opened in 1886, and arrange trackage rights over predecessor roads of the future Reading Railroad and Central of New Jersey to reach the Hudson River at Jersey City.

Garrett was offered the newly built Pittsburgh & Lake Erie in 1879 by its beleaguered investors but declined. This line fell into New York Central hands, leaving B&O to acquire its own expensive circuitous route north from Pittsburgh. In 1884, with its competitive position deteriorating and engaging in fruitless rate wars with arch-rivals PRR and NYC, revenues were overtaken by expenses. The

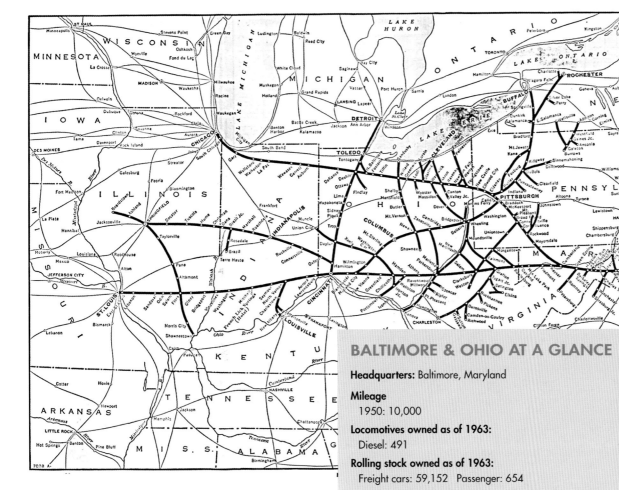

BALTIMORE & OHIO AT A GLANCE

Headquarters: Baltimore, Maryland

Mileage
1950: 10,000

Locomotives owned as of 1963:
Diesel: 491

Rolling stock owned as of 1963:
Freight cars: 59,152   Passenger: 654

Principal routes as of 1950:
Jersey City, N.J. (New York)-Baltimore, Md.-Pittsburgh,
  Pa.-Chicago
Washington, D.C.-Point of Rocks, Md.
Cumberland, Md.-Cincinnati, Ohio-St. Louis, Mo.
Detroit, Mich.-Toledo, Ohio-Cincinnati
Hamilton, Ohio-Beardstown, Ill.
Pittsburgh-Buffalo/Rochester, N.Y.
Akron-Cleveland, Ohio
Midland City, Ohio-Columbus, Ohio- Pittsburgh

Principal passenger trains (alphabetically):
Ambassador (Baltimore-Detroit)
Capitol Limited (Jersey City-Washington-Chicago)
Cincinnatian (Detroit-Cincinnati; later, Baltimore-Washing-
  ton-Cincinnati)
Columbian (Washington-Chicago)
Diplomat (Jersey City-Washington-St. Louis)
Metropolitan Special (Washington-St. Louis)
National Limited (Jersey City-Washington-St. Louis)
Royal Blue (Jersey City-Washington)
Shenandoah (Jersey City-Washington-Chicago)

depression of the early 1890s pushed the B&O into receivership in 1896. The Pennsylvania briefly gained control in 1900, but the B&O regained independence in 1908.

In 1910 the B&O board of directors hired Daniel Willard as president, a post he held until 1942. Willard is best known for his many innovations and liberal labor views. He founded the cooperative shop plan, involving joint labor/management meetings to discuss suggestions to improve the railroad—60 years before Japanese "quality circles" and participative management became vogue in American business management. He improved the property with additional track and terminals, and greatly improved the rolling stock with steel cars and large steam locomotives. Despite pressure from coal customers, Willard was, in the 1930s, one of the first railroad presidents to promote investment in diesel-electric locomotives.

B&O was one among the first to board the streamliner bandwagon, introducing the new

TOP: A system map of the B&O from a 1954 passenger timetable. Of the several railroads linking Chicago with metropolitan New York—including the Pennsylvania, New York Central and Erie—B&O had the most circuitous route and the worst grades. However, the company made the best of it, touting "Only B&O offers travel between East and West via Washington." **ABOVE RIGHT:** The first stone laid for B&O's construction in 1828 is displayed at the B&O Railroad Museum in Baltimore, Maryland.—MIKE SCHAFER.

Coal was the staple of B&O freight traffic originating in West Virginia, where the railroad operated several coal branches. On the winding line between the Ohio River at Martinsville and B&O's Cumberland-St. Louis main line at Clarksburg, West Virginia, a coal train receives assistance from two "Shark" diesels on August 9, 1951. The B&O system in West Virginia and Maryland was rife with grades requiring helper locomotives.—E. L. THOMPSON PHOTO, COLLECTION OF JAMES MISCHKE.

streamlined *Royal Blue* between Jersey City and Washington in 1935. Flagship of the B&O was the all-sleeping car Chicago-Washington-Jersey City *Capitol Limited*. The "*Cap*" and its sister coach train, the *Columbian*, were gradually streamlined in the 1940s and early 1950s, as was the Jersey City-St. Louis *National Limited*. B&O's enthusiasm for streamlining, however, was limited by finances, so many B&O passenger trains were upgraded with modernized and redeco-

rated heavyweight cars. Nonetheless, frugal B&O operated these steam-era standard cars on some of its passenger trains nearly to the end of the 1960s.

To entice passengers, B&O relied more on innovation and quality service. To B&O goes the distinction of being the first and one of the few railroads to introduce dome-car service (in 1949) to the East Coast, where clearance restrictions precluded most Eastern railroads from embracing this popular new type of pas-

BELOW: With its numerous grades and heavy coal traffic, B&O needed beefy locomotives. Among the best in that regard were its Class EM-1 2-8-8-4 articulated steam engines, three of which create their own storm clouds while moving a coal train up the Fairport branch in northeast Ohio in the mid-1950s. At Fairport Harbor on Lake Erie, the coal will be transferred to lake boats.—COLLECTION OF LOUIS A. MARRE.

RIGHT: B&O steam locomotives were replaced by diesels from a variety of builders, including Alco (which also built steam locomotives), General Motors' Electro-Motive Division (EMD) and Baldwin (another steam-turned-diesel-builder). Here, a triple-unit set of new EMD F-series freight diesels takes a grip on a coal train at Butler, Pennsylvania, in September 1952.—GORDON LLOYD, COLLECTION OF JAMES MISCHKE.

senger car. Movies aboard Amtrak trains today are commonplace, but in the mid 1960s B&O was a pioneer in the field of rolling movie theaters, showing first-run flicks aboard its key trains.

The fight for passengers—and freight—was not an easy one, particularly in markets where leviathan Pennsylvania Railroad was the major competitor—which for B&O was most routes, chief among them New York-Washington-Pittsburgh-Chicago, and New York-Washington-St. Louis. Underscoring this situation, B&O in 1958 cut all passenger service between Jersey City and home-city Baltimore, admitting defeat to parallel Pennsylvania Railroad. Nonetheless, B&O's passenger train fleet had a small but loyal following that to a degree lasted virtually to the end of B&O passenger service in 1971. That Amtrak today still operates the *Capitol Limited*, much of it on the original B&O routing east of Pittsburgh, is testimony to the great tradition long ago established by this service.

B&O maintained a high presence in Pittsburgh, Pennsylvania, where the road's Chicago-Cumberland main line junctioned with a route to Columbus and Cincinnati and with the old Buffalo, Rochester & Pittsburgh lines north to the Great Lakes. ABOVE: A Baldwin diesel road-switcher serving as a "pusher" helps a westbound transfer freight up the grade through Schenley Tunnel in Pittsburgh in April 1962.—RODNEY PETERSON, COLLECTION OF JAMES MISCHKE. RIGHT: B&O operated modest suburban-train services out of Pittsburgh, Baltimore and Washington. In this scene dating from August 1965, a pair of "Speedliners"—B&O's term for self-propelled Rail Diesel Cars (RDC's) built by the Budd Company—skim past one of Pittsburgh's steel mills with a morning commuter run bound for downtown Pittsburgh.—RON LUNDSTROM.

We're ensconced in the Appalachian Mountains in western Maryland along B&O's Baltimore-St. Louis main line as four EMD locomotives slug up Cranberry Grade with an eastbound train on September 8, 1979. At the start of the hill a few miles back at M&K Junction, West Virginia, a set of helper locomotives (out of sight at the end of the train) was added to help hoist the heavy unit-coal train to the summit at Terra Alta, Maryland. The second locomotive in this view wears the Chessie System colors that after 1972 began being applied to B&O, Chesapeake & Ohio and Western Maryland diesels.—MIKE SCHAFER.

ABOVE: A landmark B&O depot is this ornate Victorian structure at Point of Rocks, Maryland, 42 miles west of Washington Union Station. The depot sits wedged in the junction of B&O's line to Washington with the Old Main Line to Baltimore via Sykesville, Maryland. We're looking eastward in this evening scene from September 1979 as a B&O commuter train out of Washington wheels into town to deposit passengers.—MIKE SCHAFER.

BELOW: Four brand-new EMD GP38 locomotives have coupled on to a loaded "Fairmonter" coal train in the yard at Grafton, West Virginia, on a fall day in 1967 to await a highball to begin their trip east. A large amount of the coal out of the West Virginia coal fields came from Fairmont, northwest of Grafton on B&O's Grafton-Wheeling branch, and B&O trains from Fairmont mines carried the Fairmonter nickname. Much of the bounty moving east out of this region on B&O's St. Louis-Cumberland main line was "tide coal" bound for Baltimore ports. "Steam coal" was destined for domestic power plants while "metalurgical coal" was earmarked for the blast furnaces of steel mills.—JIM BOYD.

AN UNUSUAL PROVISION IN B&O's charter that prevented additional stock from being sold at less than par condemned the railroad to a highly leveraged existence and limited the railroad's ability to finance improvements. Debt leverage can boost financial performance for stockholders in good times but can be ruinous in bad. Financially for the B&O, the 20th Century was mostly bad. Prosperity eluded many railroads during the Roaring Twenties and virtually disappeared during the Great Depression. Even the lucrative traffic levels of World War II were insufficient to relieve the B&O of its crushing debt burden.

Several times, in 1938, 1944, and 1955, B&O was able to jawbone its creditors into restructuring debt to avoid bankruptcy. The crisis of the late 1950s seemed most life-threatening. After World War II, passenger traffic nearly evaporated, creating huge operating losses subsidized by freight revenues. When freight carloadings also plunged precipitously in late 1957 due to a deepening recession, spiraling losses resulted. Deferred maintenance became acute; by 1961 lack of funds to repair freight cars put 25 percent of the fleet out of service waiting for repairs.

New management under Jervis Langdon Jr. furiously cut costs, bought new locomotives, introduced unit-train coal operations, and fast freight schedules, turning huge losses into a slight profit in 1962. The railroad merger movement circled the now-profitable B&O in 1962. Many railroads, anxious to reduce redundant operations and facilities, sought merger partners to affect these economies, and B&O stockholders were courted by the Chesapeake & Ohio and New York Central in particular during a proxy fight won by C&O in early 1963.

Although a merger per se was not implemented, C&O did gain 90 percent control of B&O and brought new financing and better equipment to B&O operations. Gradually many administrative and operational functions such as passenger operations and mechanical departments were consolidated, punctuated by the 1972 debut of the new, eye-catching Chessie System logo and corporate image worn by both C&O and B&O. In 1973, B&O, C&O and B&O neighbor Western Maryland all became subsidiaries of Chessie System.

ABOVE: When inaugurated in 1947, the *Cincinnatian* was a day run between Baltimore and Cincinnati featuring streamlined Pacific-type steam locomotives pulling modernized heavyweight passenger cars. In 1950 it became a Cincinnati-Detroit train, utilizing the same equipment. Unrebuilt heavyweight cars have been mixed with the rebuilt cars on this day's *Cincinnatian*, smoking north of Dayton, Ohio, behind one of the streamlined 4-6-2's in the spring of 1952.—R. D. Acton Sr. RIGHT: Virtually unique to the B&O were its signature color-light signals, a set of which towers above the westbound *Capitol Limited* pausing at Cumberland during a late summer's evening in 1966.—Ron Lundstrom.

In 1980 Chessie System merged with Seaboard Coast Line Industries, which owned the Seaboard Coast Line and Louisville & Nashville railroads, to form CSX Transportation. Throughout this time, B&O's identity was maintained on equipment and on employee paychecks so as to preserve a substantial Maryland state tax exemption. When the cost of this separate identity was found to exceed the tax savings, the B&O was dissolved on April 30, 1987.

Financially, the B&O was so marginal that even contrarian investors avoided it. The appeal of the Baltimore & Ohio springs from its pioneer spirit, determination in the face of adversity, innovative technology, superior service, courteous employees, aesthetic equipment, and its place in American history as the country's first common-carrier railroad.

ROUTE OF THE MINUTE MAN

Boston & Maine

A New England without the venerable Boston & Maine Railroad would be like a New England without covered bridges, quaint churches and herds of dairy cows. The B&M has been a part of New England lore since June 27, 1835, when its first segment of line opened for business on a route that would eventually connect Boston with Maine—specifically Portland.

For its first three decades or so, B&M remained a small carrier of some 75 miles. That all changed when the industrial boom hit New England in the mid 19th Century. As factories—largely textile mills—sprang up, so did railway lines. Like most American railroads, the B&M grew in part by absorbing smaller upstarts such as the Boston & Lowell, which was running trains between those two Massachusetts cities, and the Fitchburg Railroad, which ran between Boston and Troy, New York.

By the turn of the century, the B&M had grown to some 2,200 route-miles—up from little more than 200 route-miles in 1883—dominating New Hampshire and northern Massachusetts while skirting eastern and northern Vermont and poking into southern Maine and northeastern New York state. Although a virtual monopoly in some of these areas, the B&M was also a welcome contact to the outside world, particularly Boston, the hub of New England and the B&M. B&M freight trains carried raw cotton, finished textiles, milk (mostly from Vermont), potatoes (from Maine), fish and lumber products while B&M passenger trains linked hundreds of rural communities "up country" from Boston, the gateway to the rest of the world. Because of the proliferating B&M lines radiating out of Boston, the railroad provided the perfect foundation for an extensive commuter-train network which thrives to this day, though under the direction of a public agency.

Sandwiched by Montreal and Boston, Vermont and New Hampshire enjoyed the services of several Boston-Montreal passenger trains operated by B&M and other carriers in the region. One of the more well-known runs, which lasted until the mid-1960s, was the *Ambassador*, which operated via Concord, New Hampshire, to White River Junction, Vermont, on the B&M, thence to Montreal on the Central Vermont and Canadian National Railways. Others were the *Alouette*, which B&M operated between Boston and Wells River, Vermont, then handed over to Canadian Pacific for forwarding to Montreal, and the *Green Mountain Flyer*, which used B&M rails to Bellows Falls, Vermont, then proceeded via the Rutland Railroad and Canadian National to Montreal.

B&M's primary corridor for intercity passenger trains was Boston-Portland via Dover, New Hampshire. Several limited-stop, named flyers plied this 115-mile line along with an ample offering of local trains. The *Kennebec*, *Flying Yankee*, *Pine Tree* and *Penobscot* were through Boston-Bangor trains operated jointly with Maine Central, whose tracks hosted these trains beyond Portland to Bangor. B&M also handled a number of Maine-bound passenger trains out of Washington, D.C., and New York, notably the *State of Maine Express*, *Bar Harbor Express* and *East Wind*. These trains came up the New Haven Railroad to Worcester, Massachusetts, where they were handed off to B&M for the trip into Maine via Ayer, Lowell and Lawrence, Massachusetts. These trains could not operate via Boston because New Haven and B&M served separate terminals in Boston proper (B&M at North Station; New Haven at South Station).

B&M dabbled in streamlining, in 1935 purchasing a little stainless-steel diesel streamliner—a near duplicate of Burlington's *Zephyr 9900*, the country's first diesel streamliner—from the Budd Company for *Flying Yankee* service and later for use on the *Minute Man*. Like many roads during the immediate post-

BOSTON & MAINE AT A GLANCE

Headquarters: Boston, Massachusetts

Mileage:
1950: 1,700   1995: 1,350

Locomotives owned as of 1963:
Diesel: 235

Rolling stock owned as of 1963:
Freight cars: 5,490   Passenger: 155

Principal routes as of 1950:
Boston-Dover, Mass.-Portland, Me.
Boston-White River Junction, Vt.
Boston, Mass.-Troy, N.Y.
Boston-Portsmouth, N.H.-Portland, Me.
Springfield, Mass.-Berlin, N.H.
Worcester-Lowell Junction, Mass.
Worcester-Gardner, Mass.
South Ashburnham, Mass.-Bellows Falls, Vt.
Dover, N.H.-Intervale, N.H.

Notable passenger trains (alphabetically):
Alouette (Boston-Montreal)
Ambassador (New York/Boston-Montreal)
Cheshire (Boston-White River Junction)
Day White Mountains (New York-Berlin, N.H.)
Flying Yankee (Boston-Bangor, Maine)
Green Mountain Flyer (Boston-Montreal)
The Gull (Boston-Halifax, N.S.)
Kennebec (Boston-Portland-Bangor)
Minute Man (Boston-Troy, N.Y.)
Montrealer/Washingtonian (Washington-Montreal)
Mountaineer (Boston-Littleton/Bethlehem, N.H.)
Pine Tree (Boston-Portland-Bangor)
Red Wing (Boston-Montreal)
State of Maine (New York-Portland)

Although the Boston & Maine had lost much of its identity under the umbrella of its new (in 1983) owner, Guilford Transportation Industries, the railroad turned 160 years old in 1995, making it one of the oldest surviving U.S. carriers featured in this book. Weather-worn 316, a General Motors' Electro-Motive Division (EMD) GP40, stands a chilly sentinel at Plainville, Connecticut, on December 16, 1992.—SCOTT HARTLEY.

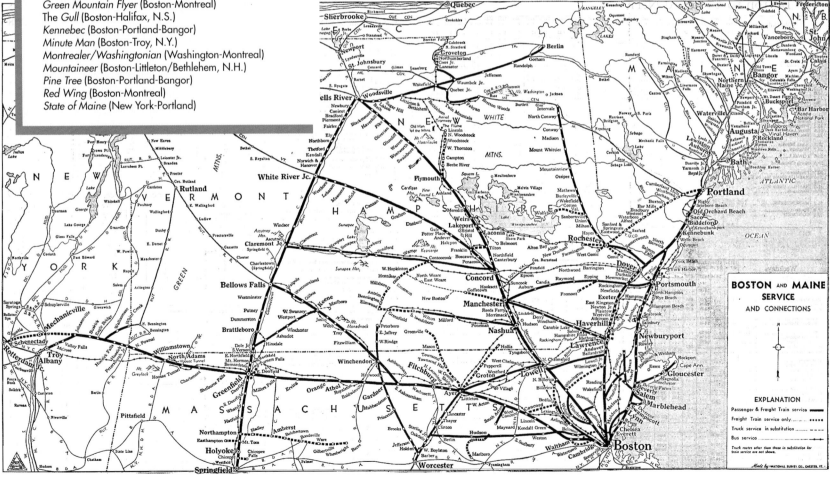

war years, B&M in 1947 further modernized its passenger trains—principally the Boston-Portland-Bangor runs—with a whole new fleet of lightweight, stainless-steel cars. In the space of a decade, B&M had become disillusioned with the passenger market, and all the lightweight cars were resold to other railroads as B&M drastically reduced its intercity service during the late 1950s, dropping it altogether by 1966. Commuter services are all that remained thereafter.

B&M's most-important freight route—the east-west main line linking Boston with the Capital Cities area of Upstate New York—ironically was a weak link in the road's passenger network, largely because parallel Boston & Albany (a New York Central affiliate) offered faster and more-direct passenger service.

B&M's star train on the route was the Boston-Troy *Minute Man*, but by 1960 all service west of Fitchburg, including the *Minute Man*, had vanished from the timetables.

This route fared much better for freight, thanks largely to the Hoosac Tunnel at North Adams, Massachusetts, in the heart of the Berkshire Hills. Officially completed in 1877, the five-mile bore took 23 years to build and cost $20 million and 195 lives. The price was indeed high for the Fitchburg, B&M's predecessor that built the tunnel, but it provided an easy-grade route over the Berkshires—something rival B&A could only wish for. In 1911 B&M electrified the route through the tunnel. The use of electric locomotives to assist trains through Hoosac greatly reduced the hazards of operating steam locomotives in

A B&M commuter train stands ready to depart for Fitchburg from track 21 at Boston's North Station circa 1950. The locomotive is a B&M Class K-7 Consolidation (2-8-0) built by the American Locomotive Company (Alco) at Schenectady, New York, in May 1910; it was scrapped in 1953. The first car on the train is a classic old B&M wooden combine (part passenger, part baggage); the remainder are steel-sheathed cars. Their clean wine-red attire makes for a handsome-looking train.—Leon Onofri, collection of Robert Willoughby Jones.

LOWER RIGHT: The date is May 7, 1950, and we're at JV Tower in Johnsonville, New York, junction of B&M's Troy branch (foreground) with the Boston-Mechanicville main line. Eastbound symbol freight MP-2 heading from Mechanicville to Portland, Maine, is in the command of a three-unit set of early Electro-Motive F-series freight locomotives clad in B&M's maroon-and-yellow paint scheme. Sturdy new diesels notwithstanding, the train had taken 35 minutes for the arduous 14-mile climb from Mechanicville.—WILLIAM D. MIDDLETON. BELOW: One of New England's most-famous rail crossroads was White River Junction in eastern Vermont. It was a junction for waterways (the White River and the Connecticut River) as well as railways (two B&M lines and the Central Vermont main line down from the Canadian border). As a rail crossroads, passenger trains at various times during the day and night congregated at WRJ's colonial depot to exchange passengers. In this scene from the summer of 1960, the north- and southbound New York-Montreal *Ambassadors* are to the left of the depot building—the B&M train facing the photographer is the southbound—while the three smoking Rail Diesel Cars (RDC's) at right constitute the joint Canadian Pacific-B&M Montreal-Boston train operating via Wells River, Vermont, and Concord, New Hampshire. The *Ambassadors* were jointly operated by B&M, CV and New Haven. The lone passenger car at left is a sleeper that will be added to the southbound *Washingtonian* in the middle of the night.—RAILROAD AVENUE ENTERPRISES.

the bore. The electrification ended in 1946 with the coming of the diesel age.

The Berkshire line—the Fitchburg Division of the B&M—became a veritable steel boulevard for freight traffic between New England and western points. Even following post-World War II freight-traffic slumps, the Fitchburg Division main line hosted as many as 16 scheduled through "symbol" freights, trains like BM-3 (Boston-Mechanicville, New York), the *Big Chief*, and MP-2 (Mechanicville-Portland), the *Forest City*.

How GOES NEW ENGLAND, so goes the B&M, and New England's slide from prosperity after World War II delivered a devastating blow to the B&M as modernization bypassed remaining frugal New England factory operations, companies moved to warmer climes, and highway competition chomped away at both freight and passenger traffic.

B&M nonetheless maintained a kind of reassuring presence in New England, its stocky steam locomotives nosing through the folds, nooks and crannies of the White Moun-

ABOVE: Symbol freight EDWH (for East Deerfield, Massachusetts-Whitefield, New Hampshire) wends lazily along the Lower Ammonoosuc River near Littleton, New Hampshire, during the summer of 1981. Paper mills in northern New Hampshire kept the B&M active in this remote portion of the Granite State.—MIKE SCHAFER.

tains to serve weathered textile factories and paper mills. Maroon diesels (later repainted blue) replaced those steam locomotives, but there were fewer customers to tend to and thus fewer trains to pull.

Eventually the situation became critical. During the late 1950s and early 1960s, under the direction of its most controversial president, Patrick McGinnis, B&M's deficits ballooned while the company took on a "deferred maintenance" approach to railroading: Spend no money on improvements and as little as possible on only the most-necessary repairs to save cash. This philosophy was shared by numerous U.S. railroads of that period, but it was a policy that could only be successful in the short term. Anything beyond, and you've wrecked the railroad. And

that's what nearly happened to the B&M.

Following several unsuccessful attempts at merger with other railroads as a means of saving itself, the B&M went bankrupt on February 1, 1970. Now B&M stood for "Bankrupt & Martyred" and, for the first few years of that decade, it appeared that the railroad would be carved up and sold to healthier connecting roads, including possibly a new mega-railroad—Consolidated Rail Corporation (Conrail)—being pieced together from a number of bankrupt Northeastern carriers. About the only happy thing to occur shortly after bankruptcy was announced was the reinstitution of intercity passenger service over a portion of the B&M. In September 1972, Amtrak revived what had been one of B&M's most important runs, the *Montrealer/Washingtonian*, using the

RIGHT: Winchendon, New Hampshire, was the crossing of two B&M local lines where each afternoon this meet occurred to exchange passengers. At left a B&M Alco RS3 has the Cheshire branch train out of Bellows Falls, Vermont, for Boston, while at right a New Haven RS3 locomotive has the Peterboro-Worcester (Massachusetts) train in tow. Despite the New Haven locomotive, both trains are B&M runs; the B&M had leased the NH diesel.—ROBERT WILLOUGHBY JONES COLLECTION.

RIGHT: On a late afternoon circa 1950, B&M's Boston engine terminal is gearing up for the commuter rush. At left is K-Class Consolidation 2394, built in 1907. At right is the 3715, one of ten Pacific-type locomotives (4-6-2 wheel arrangement) built for the B&M by Lima Locomotive Works in 1934. Although both locomotives in this scene were scrapped in 1952 and 1953 respectively, a sister engine to the 3715—B&M 3713—survives at the Steamtown museum complex at Scranton, Pennsylvania.—LEON ONOFRI COLLECTION.

B&M between Springfield, Massachusetts and White River Junction.

Fortunately, B&M got a savior in Alan B. Dustin, who stepped in as the railroad's new president and chief executive officer in 1974. For almost the next ten years, Dustin resuscitated the B&M through innovative marketing, improved infrastructure, new or rebuilt locomotives, and revamped managerial procedures. In the process, the railroad's route network underwent some interesting changes. In some cases, lines were truncated, abandoned outright, or turned over to newly formed carriers. But in a turnabout situation, B&M also wound up taking over operations on selected lines of the former New Haven Railroad such as that between Springfield and New Haven, Connecticut. Eventually the B&M's financial predicament—not to mention its traffic base—stabilized, and the railroad became a role model for regional-type railroads everywhere.

As the B&M emerged from the bankruptcy tunnel, it was purchased in whole by Guilford Transportation Industries (GTI) on June 30, 1983, for just over $24 million. Although not quite as vibrant as it was during the Dustin administration, the B&M survives in the 1990s as one of an amalgamation of three railroads operating under the GTI umbrella, including one-time B&M connections Maine Central and Springfield Terminal. All three roads share a common paint scheme, so B&M's once-familiar blue-and-white diesels no longer rustle the calm of New England villages.

In a lost corner of Massachusetts exists a marvel of 19th Century railroad engineering. The 25,081-foot Hoosac Tunnel gave B&M a shortcut through the spine of the Berkshires at Florida Mountain and a competitive edge to competitor Boston & Albany, whose main line between those two points paralleled B&M several miles to the south. Hoosac's construction began in 1851; it was opened in 1875 (although the date on the east portal in this scene says 1877, which is probably when the very final phases of construction were actually completed). The project came at great cost: $20 million and 195 lives, and reportedly there are hauntings in the tunnel area attributed to those lost souls. The west portal is near North Adams, Massachusetts, but the east portal—where an eastbound is emerging on a humid summer morning in 1974—is off on remote backroads. Hoosac remains the longest tunnel east of the Rocky Mountains, but most of the traffic on the B&M's Berkshire line has been diverted to the old B&A, now run by Conrail.—MIKE SCHAFER.

ROUTE OF THE "400"

Chicago & North Western

When it was merged into giant Union Pacific in 1995, the Chicago & North Western Railway was, at age 147, one of the oldest surviving railroads in the U.S. Here was a company whose name hadn't changed since 1859—a testament to a strength and independence not shared by all Midwestern rail carriers.

The name "Chicago" appears in numerous railroad company names, but it holds special meaning for the C&NW whose predecessor Galena & Chicago Union operated the first train out of that fledgling city behind the first locomotive— the *Pioneer*—in the city, in 1848. Railroading in the nation's rail capital hasn't been the same since.

By 1856, G&CU rails had reached Freeport, Illinois, and, on a separate line, the Mississippi River. In the late 1850s the new Chicago & Fond du Lac Railroad was building from northeastern Illinois to Upper Michigan. The C&FL was reorganized as the Chicago & North Western in 1859 and merged with the G&CU five years later. The 1866 lease of the Chicago & Milwaukee, which did indeed link those two cities, signaled the start of a trend of C&NW acquiring other roads through lease or purchase while it also built its own lines.

One of these lines was a more-or-less straight shot of iron west from Chicago to the Missouri River at Council Bluffs, Iowa, completed in 1867. It became an ideal route over which to ship supplies from the East to the then-abuilding Union Pacific, whose principal eastern terminus was Council Bluffs. When UP opened a through route to the West Coast with the driving of the Golden Spike at Promontory, Utah, in 1869, C&NW became one of the strategic links in this new Chicago-to-the-Pacific "Overland Route"—more so than C&NW management then might have ever imagined.

As the 20th Century unfolded, C&NW laced the Midwest with seemingly countless secondary and branch lines that poked and prodded into nearly all nooks and crannies of Wisconsin, Minnesota, South Dakota and Iowa. These local lines made North Western one of the archetypical granger railroads, moving astonishing amounts of corn, wheat and other agricultural products. The railroad played a prominent role in northeastern Illinois as well, particularly in Chicago, where its three major lines fanning from downtown developed into arteries critical to the movement of commuter traffic.

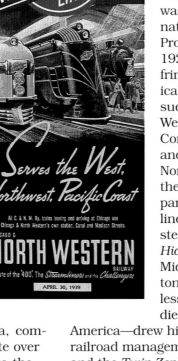

Into the early 1930s, C&NW remained the consummate—if perhaps a mite stodgy —Midwestern carrier, performing the day-to-day tasks of railroading with aplomb. About the only claim to fame the railroad had was that it held title to the nation's largest freight facility, Proviso Yard, which opened in 1929 on Chicago's western fringes. Entrenchment in America's Grain Belt did not ensure success, for by 1935 the North Western was in bankruptcy. Competitors Milwaukee Road and Burlington goaded the North Western into change in the 1930s when those two companies developed fast streamlined trains. Milwaukee Road's steam-powered streamliner *Hiawatha* captured the fancy of Mid-Americans while Burlington's revolutionary new stainless-steel *Zephyr*—the first diesel-powered streamliner in America—drew high praise from travelers and railroad management alike. The *Hiawatha* and the *Twin Zephyr*s began high-speed service between Chicago and Minneapolis/St. Paul in 1935.

Despite its financial problems, C&NW came up with a stop-gap competitive response: Using upgraded but otherwise conventional steam locomotives and rolling stock, the railroad introduced—also in 1935—the "*400*" between Chicago, Milwaukee and Minneapolis. The limited-stop train made the 400-or-so mile trip in some 400 minutes, hence the name.

Although arguably not quite as successful

FACING PAGE: General Motors and Alco diesels idle between assignments while at Chicago & North Western's Butler engine facility near Milwaukee on a summer evening in 1965.—RON LUNDSTROM. FACING PAGE INSET: Nose dents and nicks attest to years of toil for this Electro-Motive F7 freight locomotive. C&NW's streamlined diesels sported "flying saucer" nose artwork that surrounded the traditional C&NW herald.—MIKE SCHAFER. LEFT: C&NW's passenger timetable from 1939 featured an artist's rendering of the train sheds of North Western Terminal in Chicago with (left to right) the new Union Pacific-C&NW Streamliner *City of Los Angeles*, a streamlined C&NW steam locomotive and the famous "*400*".

NORTH WESTERN AT A GLANCE

Headquarters: Chicago, Illinois

Mileage
1950: 9,693   1995: 5,300

Locomotives owned as of 1963:
Diesel: 744

Rolling stock owned as of 1963:
Freight cars: 41,383   Passenger: 447

Principal lines circa 1950:

Chicago-Fremont/Omaha, Neb.
Fremont-Lander, Wyo.
Nelson, Ill.-Madison, Ill. (St. Louis)
Chicago-Minneapolis, Minn., via Madison and Wyeville, Wis.
Milwaukee, Wis.-Rapid City, S. Dak., via Wyeville, Wis., and Mankato, Minn.
Eau Claire, Wis.-Duluth, Minn.
Chicago-Milwaukee, Wis., via Kenosha, Wis.
Chicago-Milwaukee via Bain, Wis.
Milwaukee-Green Bay via Manitowoc, Wis.
Milwaukee-Green Bay via Fond du Lac, Wis.
Green Bay-Ashland, Wis., via Rinelander
Green Bay-Ishpeming, Mich.
Powers, Mich.-Hurley, Wis.
Minneapolis/St. Paul-Omaha via Mankato
Lake Crystal (Mankato)-Des Moines, Iowa

Notable passenger trains (alphabetically):

Ashland Limited (Chicago-Green Bay-Ashland)
Dakota "400" (Chicago-Madison-Huron, S. Dak.)
Duluth-Superior Limited (Chicago-Madison-Duluth)
Flambeau "400" (Chicago-Green Bay-Ashland)
Kate Shelly "400" (Chicago-Boone, Iowa)
North Western Limited (Chicago-St. Paul-Minneapolis)
Peninsula "400" (Chicago-Green Bay-Ishpeming)
Shoreland "400" (Chicago-Milwaukee-Green Bay)
Twin Cities "400" (Chicago-St. Paul-Minneapolis)
Valley "400" (Chicago-Green Bay-Menominee, Mich.)
C&NW also was a forwarder for Union Pacific's famed fleet of streamliners and Domeliners (e.g., *City of Los Angeles, City of Portland*) between Chicago and Omaha until October 1955.

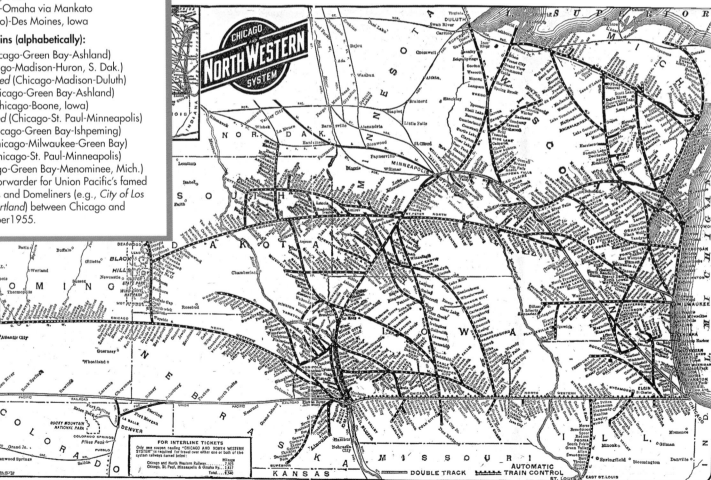

as the *Twin Zephyr* and the *Hiawatha*, the
"400" nonetheless had a significant impact on
the marketplace, so much so that within four
years the railroad could afford to re-equip it
with diesel locomotives and lightweight,
streamlined cars and give it a new name: *Twin
Cities "400."* From there, the *"400"* streamliner
concept spread to other C&NW runs, and by
mid-century the railroad had a whole fleet of
yellow-and-green *"400"*'s on most of its principal routes, the longest run being the *Dakota
"400"*, introduced in 1950 between Chicago
and Huron, South Dakota, more than 653
miles. Two *"400"*'s serving the remote vaca-
tionlands of northern Wisconsin and Upper
Michigan included the *Flambeau "400"* and
the *Peninsula "400."* The heavily populated
Chicago-Milwaukee-Green Bay corridor
included those two *"400"*'s as well as a number of other shorter-distance trains such as
the *Green Bay "400"* and *Commuter "400."*

C&NW's experience with streamlined trains

actually pre-dated the 1939 streamlining of
the original *"400"*, for in 1935 Union Pacific
introduced its first Chicago-based streamliner,
the *City of Portland*, which C&NW relayed
between Chicago and Omaha. C&NW's affiliation with UP (and indirectly Southern Pacific)
eventually resulted in joint ownership of such
nationally acclaimed streamliners as the *City
of Los Angeles*, *City of San Francisco*, *City of
Denver*, and the *Challenger*, all of which
reached Chicago via the C&NW. Meanwhile,
UP also fed a significant amount of freight
traffic to C&NW at Council Bluffs and Fremont, Nebraska, and vice versa.

Despite record freight and passenger traffic
levels and a positive cash flow ushered in by
World War II, a new postwar fleet of streamliners, and some dabbling in dieselization,
C&NW fortunes withered in the face of a
euphoric postwar America. The railroad's
decline was underscored in 1955 when UP
shifted its great streamliner fleet to the Mil-

FACING PAGE: North Western's imposing Chicago depot shown in this 1971
view that looks northwest opened in
1911. It stood at the corner of Clinton
and Madison streets a few blocks west
of the Loop until the mid-1980's when it
was replaced by a towering Art Deco
glass building. The 1911 structure was
designed by architects Frost and
Granger, both of whom were married to
daughters of C&NW's president at the
time.—MIKE SCHAFER. ABOVE: On the
other side of the stately depot building
was, of course, the train shed and
approach tracks. In this 1954 scene
looking southeast, a C&NW 4-6-2 locomotive steams away from the depot
with a string of new bilevel commuter
cars as a *"400"* streamliner also heads
out of town.—PHILIP A. WEIBLER.

BELOW: The success of the steam-powered "400" of 1935 between Chicago and the Twin Cities spawned a whole fleet of "400" streamliners serving the upper Midwest. The most far-flung was the *Dakota "400"*, which ran on an extended all-day schedule between Chicago and Huron, South Dakota, 653 miles. (For a short time in the late 1950s, the train's run was extended overnight to Rapid City, 940 miles out of Chicago.) On a May afternoon in 1954, the eastbound *Dakota "400"* cruises through the lush Wisconsin dairylands near Lodi. The train will arrive at Chicago's North Western Terminal in late evening.—WILLIAM D. MIDDLETON.

waukee Road between Omaha and Chicago. At the time, Milwaukee Road was considered the stronger of the two granger rivals.

Salvation came when Ben Heineman, was elected Chairman of the Board in 1956. The changes were swift and sweeping. Total dieselization was achieved later that year without buying another locomotive—the Heineman team simply achieved better utilization of the diesels C&NW already had. North Western poured investment into new freight facilities, including a major new car-building and repair facility at Clinton, Iowa.

The new regime agressively trimmed North Western's most-unprofitable passenger services. In 1958 many of North Western's secondary and local passenger trains serving Wisconsin were discontinued. However, through a special agreement with the State of Wisconsin, selected remaining intercity trains

such as the *Flambeau "400"* and *Peninsula "400"* were upgraded with new bilevel cars similar to those the railroad had earlier introduced to its suburban-train operations.

C&NW's Chicagoland commuter operations themselves saw changes as new money- and equipment-saving operational procedures were implemented. One of these was the "push-pull" concept whereby the locomotive pulled the train in one direction (normally out from Chicago) and on its return run pushed the train, controlled by the engineer and fireman in a special cab in the end commuter car. This arrangement saved the time and expenses involved in turning locomotives at each end of their runs.

Although it was too late to save the intercity passenger train—the famed *Twin Cities "400"* was discontinued in 1963—C&NW's suburban passenger train service did go on to

ABOVE: During the waning hours of a late fall day in 1965, a westbound freight hustles away from Dixon, Illinois, along the Rock River with a merchandise train that will be handed over to the Union Pacific in Nebraska the following day. C&NW's busy Chicago-Nebraska main line through northern Illinois and central Iowa was considered part of the "Overland Route" which also comprised UP and Southern Pacific.—MIKE SCHAFER. LEFT: Two burly Fairbanks-Morse diesels schlep along near Lake Forest, Illinois, in Chicago's northern suburbs with a freight out of Milwaukee in March 1964. C&NW maintained a respectable fleet of diesels from builder FM, located on-line at Beloit, Wisconsin. This scene also illustrates a C&NW anomaly: left-hand running on double-track main line. Most U.S. railroads favored the traditional right-hand running.—TERRY NORTON.

BELOW LEFT: Under the looming countenance of the Wisconsin state capitol in Madison, the annual *Circus Parade Limited* heads for Chicago's northern suburbs and ultimately Milwaukee in 1982. The authentic circus train originated at Baraboo, Wisconsin, home of the famous Circus World Museum. BELOW: In typical granger fashion, C&NW fielded branch lines throughout the Midwest. In June 1971, a single diesel tiptoes over bumpy track at Mount Horeb, Wisconsin, during its trek with a branchline freight through southwestern Wisconsin.—BOTH PHOTOS, MIKE SCHAFER.

become one of the first (and perhaps only) suburban rail passenger operations in the nation to boast a profit, in the mid 1960s.

Also in 1958, C&NW entered an era of renewed growth when it absorbed the 44-mile Litchfield & Madison, giving C&NW its own entrance into metropolitan St. Louis. In 1960 C&NW merged with the 1,400-mile Minneapolis & St. Louis and in 1968 absorbed another 1,400-mile carrier, the Chicago Great Western, as well as shortlines Des Moines & Central Iowa and Fort Dodge, Des Moines &

Southern. During the 1960s, the UP was eyeing the Chicago, Rock Island & Pacific (yet another carrier with a Chicago-Omaha main line) to be its new gateway to Chicago— through outright purchase if possible. C&NW fought this proposal vigorously.

North Western's decade of growth was soon offset in the 1970s by the abandonment of hundreds of miles of unprofitable branch and secondary main lines. Slowly, C&NW rebuilt itself into a "lean and mean" carrier—and UP eventually decided to return to its partnership

with the North Western and forget about the Rock Island. In due time, C&NW and UP coordinated and restrengthened east-west through-freight operations, harkening to the time when UP-C&NW cooperated with Overland streamliner operations. The hot trains on C&NW's Chicago-Nebraska main line were no longer the *City of Los Angeles* and *City of San Francisco*; in the 1970s and 1980's it was the *Falcons*, scheduled piggyback trains linking Chicago with the West Coast.

The Rock Island stopped operations altogether in 1980. C&NW picked up pieces of the Rock it felt would be strategic additions, and as the 1980's unfolded, the long-historic UP-C&NW alliance had found new vigor.

This alliance, in fact, was key to one of North Western's most significant triumphs of the late 20th Century: the construction of a new route to Wyoming's Powder River coal basin. Opened in 1984, the new line became the state-of-the-art rail artery for UP-C&NW coal trains. The Powder River coal line was North Western's last big adventure. In 1995, what some railroad historians and analysts have long said was inevitable happened: Chicago & North Western was merged into Union Pacific.

C&NW moved a respectable amount of ore out of the iron ranges of northern Wisconsin and Upper Michigan. Michigan's Upper Peninsula is ablaze with color as a loaded ore train moves east along Goose Lake on C&NW's line between Ishpeming and Powers, Michigan, in September 1986. At Escanaba, Michigan, the ore will be transferred to Great Lakes ore boats. The three brutish locomotives heading up the unit-ore train are 2750-hp. Century-series units from Alco. They were originally owned by Norfolk & Western; power-short C&NW purchased them secondhand in the 1970s.—STEVE SMEDLEY.

ABOVE: Critical to North Western's success during its final years as an independent carrier was the capture of coal traffic emanating from Wyoming's Powder River coal basin. Working with future merger partner Union Pacific, C&NW operated thousands of Powder River coal trains throughout the 1980s and into the 1990s. In this 1994 vista of downtown St. Paul, two new C&NW General Electric locomotives ease a Dairyland Coal train eastward along the Mississippi River toward a power plant in neighboring Wisconsin.—STEVE GLISCHINSKI.

RIGHT: C&NW maintained a fairly high profile in the corporate world in regard to its coal business, often dispatching special business trains to carry potential investors over C&NW—and sometimes UP—property. Looking much like a revived "400" streamliner of yore, one such train is shown winding through the coal country near Bill, Wyoming, in 1987. C&NW assembled its business train by acquiring surplus passenger cars from other railroads (as well as few from its own stock) and heavily revamping them with luxurious guestrooms, conference rooms and lounge and dining areas.—MIKE SCHAFER.

The "Chicago" in Chicago & North Western was for good reason: Not only was it the railroad's hometown, but C&NW predecessor Galena & Chicago Union operated the first train out of Chicago in 1848 behind a spindly little steam locomotive (the first to operate in the city of Chicago) named *The Pioneer*. Well over 120 years later, on May 15, 1980, a pair of C&NW's then-newest locomotives—GP50's Nos. 5050 and 5051, freshly outshopped from Electro-Motive Division of General Motors—poses for their portrait with the world's tallest building, Chicago's Sears Tower, looming in the background.—STEVE SMEDLEY.

Chicago, Burlington & Quincy

The Burlington was nearly all things to all people who had ties to railroading. Chicago, Burlington & Quincy's network of freight trains provided highly reliable transportation of goods and agricultural products. With its fleet of remarkable *Zephyr*s, Burlington was a leader in intercity passenger service—not to mention modern suburban services: CB&Q carried thousands of commuters daily in and out of Chicago. And, with its high profile and panache for public relations, Burlington was a friend to thousands of communities in the Midwest, West and South Central U.S.

All this from humble beginnings. Genesis of the CB&Q was the 12-mile Aurora Branch Railroad, formed in 1849 to link Aurora, Illinois, with the Galena & Chicago Union Railroad (later Chicago & North Western) at Turner Junction (now West Chicago), Illinois. In 1852 the little road was renamed the Chicago & Aurora, although its next step wasn't to build between its namesake cities. Rather, the C&A headed southwesterly from Batavia through Aurora to Mendota, Illinois, to meet up with the Illinois Central, which was building a north-south line through the state. In 1855, the railroad was again renamed, this time to Chicago, Burlington & Quincy. In essence that name would endure for the next 115 years, but the final extremities of CB&Q would reach well beyond Burlington, Iowa, and Quincy, Illinois.

Like other fledgling systems of its ilk, much of Burlington's early growth involved the stewardship and eventual purchase of numerous upstart companies—companies with such varied names (and goals) as the Peoria & Oquawka (Peoria to the Mississippi River), the Central Military Tract Railroad (Mendota-Galesburg, Illinois) and the Northern Cross (Galesburg-Quincy). Through these acquisitions, the CB&Q marched west to the Mississippi. Bridges over the Mississippi were opened at Burlington and Quincy in 1868.

Meanwhile, back at the east end of the railroad, the CB&Q had opened its own line from Aurora to Chicago in 1864, ending its trackage-rights operation to Chicago over competitor G&CU east of Turner Junction. Could the original builders of this 38-mile extension into the future nation's railroad capital have ever imagined the future of this line? Today it is a triple-track showcase corridor for the new (in 1995) Burlington Northern Santa Fe Corporation, hosting more than 100 high-speed freight and passenger movements a day.

During the 1860s and 1870s, the CB&Q and its affiliates sprawled across Iowa, Nebraska, and Missouri. Service to Kansas City, Missouri, and Council Bluffs, Iowa, began in 1869; to Lincoln in 1870 and Omaha in 1871. In 1882, the Burlington's extension to Denver opened for business.

What would become one of the railroad's most important routes—Chicago to the Twin Cities—would not open until 1886. But with this in place, Burlington reached important connecting railroads at Minneapolis and St. Paul, notably James J. Hill's Great Northern Railway and the Northern Pacific, another Hill interest.

In 1894 the Burlington reached St. Louis—the all-important gateway to the Southwest—and Huntley, Montana, which was the connecting point with the Northern Pacific Railway east of Billings, Montana. The Huntley line passed through Wyoming coal fields that in the late 20th Century would provide a boom for railroads that served the territory, particularly CB&Q successor Burlington Northern.

The importance of the CB&Q to Hill's railroads could not be overstated. The Burlington was the perfect link to Chicago and all the Eastern carriers that terminated there, and it also would give GN and NP numerous gateways to America's bread belt. Thus, in 1901, the CB&Q was sold to (but not merged with) Hill's GN and NP. Now Hill eyed Texas and the

FACING PAGE: While savoring the verdant Rock River Valley at Oregon, Illinois, in June 1965, nature-lover Joyce Norton also pays homage to No. 97, the hottest freight train on CB&Q's high-speed main line between Aurora, Illinois, and the Twin Cities. Westbound 97 was a Chicago-Seattle run jointly operated by CB&Q and Great Northern; the latter handled the train west of the Twin Cities.—TERRY NORTON. FACING PAGE INSET: Stainless steel was synonymous with Burlington's passenger-train fleet, and many of the road's passenger cars were named, with "Silver" used as a prefix. Cars with evocative names like *Silver Veranda, Silver Lookout* and *Silver Cuisine* carried passengers destined for CB&Q points "Everywhere West."—MIKE SCHAFER. LEFT: CB&Q's passenger timetable covers changed little during the 1940's, 1950's, and early 1960's. Nearly all featured this nose-on view of a *Zephyr* train being pulled by a set of CB&Q's pre-war General Motor's (EMD) stainless-steel sheathed E5 locomotives.

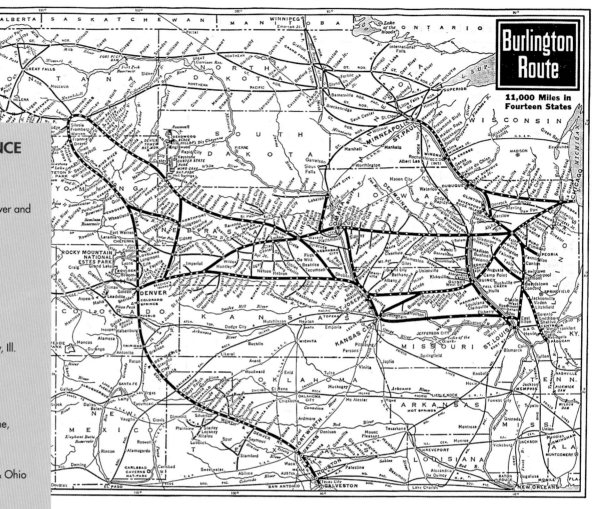

BURLINGTON ROUTE AT A GLANCE

Headquarters: Chicago, Illinois

Mileage

1950: 11,000 (includes subsidiaries Fort Worth & Denver and Colorado & Southern)

Locomotives owned as of 1963:

Steam: 10   Diesel: 691

Rolling stock owned as of 1963:

Freight cars: 41,099   Passenger cars: 925

Principal lines circa 1950:

Aurora, Ill.-Minneapolis, Minn., via Rochelle, Ill.
Chicago-Omaha-Denver via Lincoln, Neb.
Galesburg, Ill.-Kansas City/St. Joseph, Mo., via Quincy, Ill.
Savanna/Rock Island, Ill.-Paducah, Ky.
Burlington, Iowa-St. Louis via Quincy
Omaha-Kansas City via St. Joseph
Napier, Mo. (St. Joseph)-Oxford, Neb.
Table Rock, Neb.-Billings, Mont., via Lincoln
Billings-Galveston, Texas, via Thermopolis and Cheyenne, Wyo., and Denver
Ashland, Neb.-Sioux City, Iowa
Galesburg-Peoria, Ill.
Kansas City-St. Louis (trackage rights on Gulf, Mobile & Ohio Kansas City-Mexico, Mo.)

Notable passenger trains (alphabetically):

Afternoon Zephyr (Chicago-Twin Cities)
Ak-Sar-Ben Zephyr (Chicago-Lincoln)
American Royal Zephyr (Chicago-Kansas City)
Black Hawk (Chicago-Twin Cities)
California Zephyr (Chicago-Oakland, California; jointly operated with Rio Grande and Western Pacific)
Denver Zephyr (Chicago-Denver-Colorado Springs)
Empire Builder (Chicago-Seattle/Portland, operated jointly with Great Northern and Spokane, Portland & Seattle)
Exposition Flyer (Chicago-Oakland, California; jointly operated with Rio Grande and Western Pacific; replaced by *California Zephyr* in 1949)
Kansas City Zephyr (Chicago-Kansas City)
Mainstreeter (Chicago-Seattle/Portland, operated jointly with Northern Pacific and Spokane, Portland & Seattle)
Morning Zephyr (Chicago-Twin Cities)
Nebraska Zephyr (Chicago-Lincoln)
North Coast Limited (Chicago-Seattle/Portland, operated jointly with Northern Pacific and Spokane, Portland & Seattle)
Pioneer Zephyr (West Quincy-Hannibal, Mo.)
Sam Houston Zephyr (Dallas-Houston)
Texas Zephyr (Denver-Dallas)
Western Star (Chicago-Seattle/Portland, operated jointly with Great Northern and Spokane, Portland & Seattle)
Zephyr Rocket (Minneapolis-St. Louis; jointly operated with Rock Island)

Gulf of Mexico, and he reached those goals in 1908 by having his CB&Q acquire, as subsidiaries, the Colorado & Southern and its affiliate Fort Worth & Denver City.

In a quest for coal to sustain its growing steam locomotive fleet, Burlington early in the 1900s extended itself into southern Illinois coal country and finally to the Ohio River in 1910. At virtually the opposite end of the railroad in 1914, Burlington opened an extension from the NP southwest of Billings to the C&S at Orin Junction, Wyoming. With this in place, Burlington Route growth in terms of breadth and width had just about reached its peak. From here on, growth would largely be in terms of traffic and technological development.

From the start, Burlington was a strong railroad, and it weathered World War I and the Depression better than many of its contemporaries. Much of Burlington's success during the first half of the 20th Century can be attributed to the visionary Ralph Budd, who left the Great Northern to become president of the Burlington in 1932—CB&Q's worst year in terms of traffic and earnings. Budd was one of the few rail industry leaders of that period who realized that, in the face of rapidly expanding highways, the railroads no longer held a monopoly on American transportation,

and that if the railroads wanted business, they would have to work for it through modernization and service, the Depression notwithstanding.

Under Budd, that's just what the Burlington did. One of Budd's most-significant accomplishments was the *Zephyr* project. During his years on the GN, Budd had been impressed by the reliability and economy of the stationary diesel engines used by GN in building its Cascade Tunnel in the late

SILVER KING IN SHOP
I.O. 10137

No 597

ABOVE: The finishing touches are being applied to the power car for the new *Denver Zephyr* under construction at the EMD plant in LaGrange in 1935. From 1934 to 1939, *Zephyr* power units featured this "shovelnose" design.—COLLECTION OF MIKE SCHAFER. LEFT: From the 1934 *Zephyr 9900* to the 1956 *Denver Zephyr,* all new rolling stock built expressly for *Zephyr* service was manufactured by the Edward G. Budd Company near Philadelphia. This 1948 view at Aurora shows the 1936 edition of the *Denver Zephyr* arriving from its namesake city.—W. REUGGER, CALS CLASSICS.

ABOVE: Proud of its past and knowing the value of public relations, CB&Q never hesitated to show the world what steam locomotion was all about, running numerous steam-powered excursion trains in the Midwest from the late 1950s until 1966 when new management ended Q's popular steam program. The Q maintained a small cadre of steamers for excursion service, the star of which was the 5632, a Class O-5 Northern (4-8-4) of impressive dimensions. The Northern is shown at speed near Trempeleau, Wisconsin, on October 4, 1959, with a special train sponsored by the Minnesota Railfans' Association.—WILLIAM D. MIDDLETON.

1920s. With this in mind, Budd collaborated with General Motors' Electro-Motive Corporation on developing a diesel engine suitable for locomotion. EMC did just that, and the new engine was placed within the *Zephyr*, whose construction was already under way at the Edward G. Budd Company in Philadelphia.

The stainless-steel *Zephyr*, No. 9900, rolled out of the shops in April 1934 and immediately barnstormed 30 Eastern cities. After it was delivered to CB&Q on May 11, it toured the Burlington system, exhibiting at 16 on-line cities. Then, on May 26 of that year, the *Zephyr* made history with a nonstop, dawn-to-dusk run from Denver right into the Century of Progress exposition at Chicago. Finally, in November, the *Zephyr* entered regular service between Kansas City and Lincoln.

Besides being one of America's earliest streamliners, *Zephyr 9900* was the first successful application of diesel power to over-the-

road rail transport. The diesel era that revolutionized railroading in mid-century can thus be traced to the Chicago, Burlington & Quincy. Burlington's original *Zephyr* was a symbol of renaissance not only for the CB&Q, but for America's railroads as a whole.

So successful was *Zephyr 9900* that Burlington began ordering a whole fleet of *Zephyr*s to upgrade (and economize) passenger operations. In 1935, the *Twin Zephyr*s entered service between Chicago and Minneapolis while the *Mark Twain Zephyr* began rolling between Burlington and St. Louis. In 1936 the *Denver Zephyr* began linking Chicago and Denver, while the *Ozark State Zephyr* began serving Kansas City and St. Louis.

"Zephyrization" continued after World War II with new rolling stock, including another Burlington innovation which would revolutionize passenger-train travel all over North America: the Vista-Dome car. CB&Q is attributed to building the first successful dome car, which CB&Q did at its Aurora shops in 1945 by modifying a pre-war stainless-steel light-weight coach. The dome concept, which allowed passengers a 360-degree view of the countryside from a glass-enclosed upper-level seating area, was quickly embraced by all the major passenger-car manufacturers, and by the 1950's "domeliners" were proliferating throughout the Midwest and West.

One of the most celebrated of these new-age domeliners was the *California Zephyr*, inaugurated in 1949 by Burlington, Rio Grande, and Western Pacific. The highly successful Chicago-Oakland train still operates, albeit with all-new equipment operated under the banner of Amtrak.

LEFT: CB&Q's early "hood"-type (non-streamlined) diesels wore a handsome paint scheme of black and gray with red and yellow accent striping. A local freight with one of the early-scheme units switches at Mendota, Illinois, circa 1963. BELOW: A Galesburg-bound freight out of Chicago crosses the Illinois Central and Milwaukee Road at Mendota during the winter of 1965-66. Guarding the intersection of these three railroads was the "leaning tower of Mendota."—BOTH PHOTOS, JIM BOYD.

In addition to the *Zephyr*s, the "Q" maintained a sort of "joint custody" of various GN and NP transcontinental trains, which ran through to Chicago over CB&Q's scenic Mississippi River route. Thus famous flyers like the *Empire Builder* and *North Coast Limited*, while closely associated with GN and NP, were very much Burlington trains too.

Burlington's multitude of successes in the passenger field weren't limited to the long-distance traveler. CB&Q was the first of several Chicago-area railroads to embrace the bilevel passenger car concept emerging in the late 1940's, and in 1950 the first bilevel, high-capacity commuter cars entered service on Q's Chicago-Aurora route. That these original cars have remained in suburban service for nearly half a century, and that virtually all Chicago suburban-train service is now han-

dled by bilevel cars is testament to another pioneering Burlington achievement.

CB&Q's ACCOMPLISHMENTS certainly weren't limited to the passenger field. The CB&Q-D&RGW-WP alliance of *California Zephyr* fame actually predated the *CZ*'s appearance by 17 years: In 1934 the trio established reliable through freight service between Chicago and California. In 1940, CB&Q began applying the relatively new truck trailer-on-flatcar concept—piggyback, as it would become popularly known after World War II—to the Chicago-Kansas City route.

Despite the introduction of diesel power in 1934, steam was still king on Burlington freight trains well into World War II. Central to Burlington's fleet of modern mainline steam power were a fleet of 36 Northern-type (4-8-4

BELOW: More than 11,000 hp. in the form of five EMD locomotives heads this 100-car ore train near Savanna on September 1, 1964. The 8,500-ton train originated on the Great Northern in Minnesota; in the Twin Cities, GN handed the train over to CB&Q, which moved it south along its scenic Mississippi River line—"Where Nature Smiles for 300 Miles", as CB&Q travel ads for the *Twin Zephyr*s once touted.—JIM BOYD.

wheel arrangement) locomotives constructed between 1930 and 1940, some of them at Burlington's own shops in West Burlington, Iowa.

But with Ralph Budd's penchant for economies and reliability of diesel power, it did not take long for Burlington to enter a planned dieselization program. The first switching diesels had been delivered in the 1930s, and the first road-freight diesels—streamlined-cab units from Electro-Motive—were delivered during World War II. By the end of the 1950s, the Burlington was fully dieselized—save for one steam locomotive in freight service on subsidiary C&S until 1962 and a handful of steam locomotives maintained for excursion service until 1966. In fact, early in the 1960's, CB&Q began replacing its first-generation diesels with more-modern diesel power.

The flexibility and standardization of diesel power led to an expansion of jointly operated through-freight services among various U.S.

TOP: CB&Q was one of the very few U.S. carriers that had some of its passenger diesels sheathed in stainless-steel fluting to match *Zephyr* rolling stock. The results were striking, as evidenced in this scene of the Chicago-Minneapolis *Morning Zephyr* making its brief pause for passengers at Oregon, Illinois, circa 1964. A set of E5-type Electro-Motive diesels built just prior to World War II lead the shimmering domeliner.—JIM BOYD. CB&Q is also credited with designing the first successful dome car, which it did in 1945 by outfitting a 1940-built lightweight stainless-steel coach with an upper-level, glass-enclosed seating area. The car served as a prototype for carbuilder Budd Company, which subsequently outshopped dozens of "Vista-Dome" cars for a number of U.S. and Canadian railroads. This is the interior of a dome coach on the Burlington-Rio Grande-Western Pacific *California Zephyr*, introduced in 1949.—MIKE SCHAFER.

ABOVE: Burlington's sizeable fleet of F-type freight locomotives from EMD were built in the years immediately following World War II. They wore a scheme of light gray accented by red-and-black stripe designs. Often called "graybacks" by CB&Q historians, two sets of the venerable diesels stand vigil at Galesburg, Illinois, on a fall evening in 1965. Within a few years, this veteran locomotive style would be largely retired as new locomotives were delivered.—JIM BOYD.
RIGHT: Burlington operated a first-rate suburban service between Chicago Union Station and Aurora, 38 miles. Because the main line between those two points was mostly triple track and equipped with strategically located crossover tracks and Centralized Traffic Control, CB&Q and successor Burlington Northern were able to run their commuter trains fast and frequent. When Q's passenger diesels weren't assigned to a *Zephyr*, they usually took a turn with a suburban train, such as this afternoon run leaving Chicago.—MIKE SCHAFER.

railroads, but Burlington was somewhat of a pioneer in this realm as well. In the 1960's, CB&Q had "run-through" freight-train operations with Great Northern, Rio Grande, Union Pacific, New York Central and Erie Lackawanna, so it was not uncommon to see the diesels of those roads on CB&Q tracks.

RALPH BUDD RETIRED from the Burlington in 1949. He was replaced by Harry C. Murphy, who held many of the same convictions as Budd. Through Murphy's leadership, the spirit and determination of the Burlington, as well as its warm "hometown" personality—a rarity in railroads today—glowed well into 1960's.

Murphy led the railroad in more development and improvements, one of the most significant being the Centennial Cutoff, which in 1952 shortened the Chicago-Kansas City route by 22 miles and greatly speeded up freight and passenger schedules between the city pair. In 1957-58, the railroad's main freight facility in Chicago, Clyde Yard, was transformed from a "flat-switching" yard to a "hump" operation whereby cars were rolled by gravity into their respective tracks via electronically controlled retarder tracks and switches. As one of the first railroads to adopt the highly efficient Centralized Traffic Control in 1927, the Q by 1965 boasted some 1,750 miles of CTC-operated routes.

Even in the face of increasing passenger deficits following World War II, the Murphy administration moved forward in the passenger field, introducing the Vista-Dome *Kansas City Zephyr* and *American Royal Zephyr* on the new high-speed route to K.C. in 1953 and re-equipping the *Denver Zephyr* in 1956.

Following Murphy's retirement in 1965, subsequent management readied the CB&Q for its long-planned merger with GN, NP and Spokane, Portland & Seattle. This event, a dream of James J. Hill and others since the early part of the 20th Century, finally occurred on March 2, 1970, with the formation of the Burlington Northern Railroad. BN would last a quarter of a century, merging with giant Santa Fe on September 22, 1995, to form the Burlington Northern Santa Fe Corporation. Again, the "Burlington" name survived as did perhaps a little of that CB&Q spirit. After all, *Zephyr*s still ply some of BNSF's earliest CB&Q routes.

Burlington was a modern railroad always on the cutting edge of innovation, but it also had a dash of good old Midwestern frugality and a penchant for keeping its physical plant—regardless of its age—in top-notch condition. **UPPER AND LOWER LEFT:** The *California Zephyr*—itself a postwar "baby boomer"—meets CB&Q's 4960—a 2-8-2 type steam locomotive built in 1918 and still earning revenues (and p.r. points) in 1966 hauling excursionists. —TWO PHOTOS, MIKE SCHAFER. **BELOW:** Another holdover of the early 20th Century, this classic wooden caboose belonging to Burlington subsidiary Fort Worth & Denver managed to linger in freight service well into the 1960s along with many other wooden Burlington cabooses. This veteran was trailing FW&D train 176 leaving Lubbock, Texas, in April 1964.—JOE MCMILLAN.

AMERICA'S RESOURCEFUL RAILROAD

Chicago, Milwaukee, St. Paul & Pacific

The Milwaukee Road long had a close association to granger America, which it blanketed with a network of main routes and branch lines. But it was also a transcontinental railroad, stretching from central Indiana and Chicago all the way to the Pacific Northwest via the Twin Cities—Minneapolis and St. Paul.

Its official name for most of its life was the Chicago, Milwaukee, St. Paul & Pacific. As its popularized name "Milwaukee Road" implies, Wisconsin's largest city was the railroad's principal hub, and though more traffic was handled at nearby Chicago, Milwaukee was the greatest on-line source of traffic for the railroad. In fact, Milwaukee was where the railroad was born, in 1847.

Its primordial start was as the Milwaukee & Mississippi Railroad, which began building west from Milwaukee in 1850, reaching the Mississippi River in 1857. The M&M later became the Milwaukee & Prairie du Chien which was acquired by a railroad known as the Milwaukee & St. Paul, which had built a line (under the name La Crosse & Milwaukee) from Milwaukee to La Crosse, Wisconsin. In 1874 the M&StP had been renamed Chicago, Milwaukee & St. Paul to reflect its extension to Chicago, America's new and important rail center, and to St. Paul.

By the turn of the century, the CM&StP reached out to Omaha and Kansas City and well into Minnesota, with many lines throughout northern Illinois, Iowa and Wisconsin. That wasn't far enough, though, and Milwaukee Road officials decided it was time to head for the Pacific Coast. The railroad did this by building an extension to Seattle and Tacoma via Butte, Montana, which it opened in 1909—after which "Pacific" was added to the railroad's official name. Over 650 miles of this extension was electrified in 1915, making the Milwaukee one of the few principal U.S. railroads to operate electric-powered freight and passenger trains over extensive segments

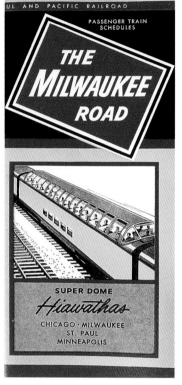

of main line. (Most electric rail operations in North America were and are for short-haul commuter-type passenger services.)

Although the Milwaukee Road skirted financial disaster off and on during the early part of this century, the line became a respectable property known for its resourcefulness. The Milwaukee was a pioneer in many respects, particularly high-speed service. In 1935 it introduced the *Hiawatha*, one of the nation's first streamlined passenger trains, between Chicago, Milwaukee and the Twin Cities.

The *Hiawatha*'s distinctive lightweight cars were built by the railroad's famed Milwaukee Shops. Although the mid-1930s were the dawn of the diesel age, the *Hiawatha* was pulled by a new streamlined steam locomotive that featured shrouding to blend with the train's smooth lines and classy orange, gray and maroon exterior. The *Hiawatha* could cruise at speeds in excess of 100 mph with nary a drop of coffee being spilled from cups in its world-class dining car.

Milwaukee Road rails served a territory steeped in Indian lore, so the Indian theming was a natural, and eventually the railroad fielded a whole fleet of *Hiawatha* streamliners serving nearly all major points of the system. So well received were the *Hiawatha*s, that they were frequently upgraded with new equipment as late as 1952.

Heart of the Milwaukee Road was its extensive shop complex in the Menomonee River valley immediately southwest of Milwaukee's business district. For years, Milwaukee Shop forces built the railroad's army of freight and passenger rolling stock (most railroads relied on outside car-building companies to construct passenger and freight cars) and performed heavy repairs and and even major rebuild work to its steam and diesel locomotive fleet. Much of the railroad's home-built freight and passenger equipment bore ribbed sides, which became the railroad's trade-

FACING PAGE: Milwaukee Road was a proud carrier that lasted for well over a century. In this 1970 scene photographed in the middle of the night at Portage, Wisconsin, a Chicago-bound manifest freight (left in photo) led by modern General Motors locomotives stops to change engine crews. At right, fast mail and express train No. 57 pauses for a similar crew change and to load and unload mail, express and other parcels before continuing its overnight dash between Chicago and Minneapolis. FACING PAGE INSET: Reminders of the dearly departed Milwaukee Road remained visible nearly a decade after it had been sold to the Soo Line. The sign was photographed at Davenport, Iowa, in 1994.—SCOTT MUSKOPF. LEFT: A Milwaukee Road public timetable from 1966 touts the railroad's famous *Hiawatha* passenger-train fleet, which served such major cities as Chicago, Milwaukee, St. Paul, Seattle and Omaha.

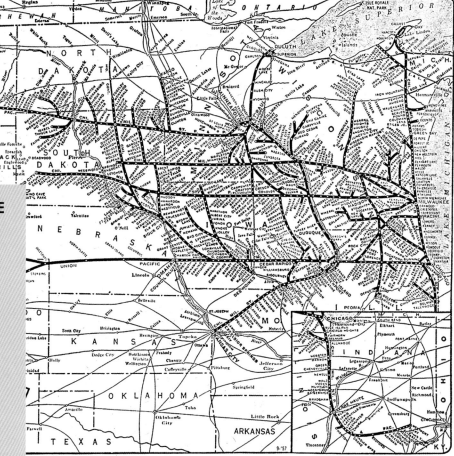

MILWAUKEE ROAD AT A GLANCE

Headquarters: Chicago, Illinois

Mileage:
1950: 10,664

Locomotives owned as of 1963:
Diesel: 803   Electric: 93

Rolling stock owned as of 1963:
Freight cars: 42,325   Passenger: 588

Principal lines as of 1950:
Chicago-Minneapolis via Milwaukee and Columbus, Wis.
New Lisbon-Woodruff, Wis.
Minneapolis-Seattle/Tacoma via Spokane, Wash.
Minneapolis/St. Paul-Calmar, Iowa, via Austin, Minn.
La Crescent, Minn.-Wessington Springs, S. Dak.
Rondout, Ill. (Chicago)-Madison, Wis.
Watertown, Wis.-Rapid City, S. Dak.
Chicago-Omaha
Manilla, Iowa-Sioux Falls, S. Dak.
Marion-Ottumwa, Iowa
Sturtevant, Wis.-Kansas City
La Crosse, Wis.-Sabula, Iowa
Des Moines-Spencer, Iowa
Chicago-Terre Haute, Ind.
Milwaukee-Ontonagon, Mich., via Green Bay, Wis.

Notable passenger trains (alphabetically):
Afternoon Hiawatha (Chicago-Milwaukee-St. Paul/Minneapolis)
Arrow (Chicago-Omaha/Sioux Falls)
Chippewa-Hiawatha (Chicago-Channing, Mich.)
Columbian (Chicago-Twin Cities-Seattle/Tacoma)
Copper Country Limited (Chicago-Green Bay-Calumet, Mich.,
   joint with Duluth, South Shore & Atlantic Railroad)
Midwest Hiawatha (Chicago-Omaha/Sioux Falls)
Morning Hiawatha (Chicago-Milwaukee-Minneapolis)
Olympian (Chicago-Twin Cities-Seattle/Tacoma)
Olympian Hiawatha (Chicago-Twin Cities-Seattle/Tacoma;
   replaced *Olympian*)
Pioneer Limited (Chicago-Milwaukee-St. Paul/Minneapolis)
Sioux (Chicago-Madison-Rapid City, S. Dak.)
Southwest Limited (Milwaukee/Chicago-Kansas City)
Tomahawk (Chicago-Minocqua, Wis.)
Varsity (Chicago-Madison)
From 1955 to 1971, Milwaukee Road also operated the
   Omaha-Chicago leg of Union Pacific's fleet of "Overland"
   streamliners including the *City of Denver, City of Portland, City
   of Los Angeles, City of San Francisco,* and the *Challenger.*

ABOVE: The Milwaukee Road dieselized most of its operations in the 1940s and 1950s largely with locomotives built by the Electro-Motive Division of General Motors and Fairbanks, Morse & Company. At Marquette, Iowa, in 1977, an FM switch engine takes a break from switching duties.—MIKE SCHAFER. TOP: CMStP&P map from 1960.

mark—although the true purpose of ribbing was to provide added strength to cars.

Like many other railroads of its class, Milwaukee began dabbling in dieselization before the U.S. became entrenched in World War II and wartime restrictions greatly slowed diesel construction. Steam locomotives finally vanished from the Milwaukee in the mid-1950s when the railroad fully dieselized all but its electrified lines in Montana, Idaho and Washington. There, electric locomotives—some of them dating from 1915—would continue to pull trains until 1974 when the electrification was deemed too costly to maintain or replace.

Like nearly all other U.S. railroads during the postwar years, Milwaukee Road passenger service took a serious blow from competing forms of transportation. One bright spot in the Milwaukee's passenger arena was the 1955 shift of Union Pacific's stable of celebrated Domeliners—famed transcons like the *City of Los Angeles, City of San Francisco* and *City of Denver*—from Chicago & North Western rails to Milwaukee Road rails between Chicago and Council Bluffs. Those newcomers, together with the railroad's own homebred passenger trains—particularly the *Hiawatha*s—had such a well-established reputation that the railroad maintained a respectable passenger operation right up until May 1, 1971, when the National Railroad Passenger Corporation—Amtrak—took

BELOW: Mainline steam power on the Milwaukee Road is well represented in this scene of Class S-2 No. 208—a Northern type (4-8-4) locomotive—wheeling through Columbus, Wisconsin, on a June afternoon in 1949. The train is en route from Chicago to the Twin Cities.—WILLIAM D. MIDDLETON.

ABOVE: Cruising toward St. Paul and Minneapolis, the *Morning Hiawatha* curves through the scenic Dells area of central Wisconsin in the summer of 1970. The Chicago-to-Twin Cities route was the first to host a *Hiawatha* streamliner (in 1935), making Milwaukee Road one of the first railroads in the U.S. to feature regularly scheduled streamlined passenger train service.— MIKE SCHAFER. RIGHT: The 1939 edition of the *Twin Cities Hiawatha* featured Hudson-type (4-6-4) locomotives shrouded in Art Deco contours. Ribbing on the tender and the passenger cars added to the racy look of the new speedster.—MIKE KEIM.

over most intercity passenger train operations in the U.S. Meanwhile, the railroad continued to operate an extensive suburban service out of Chicago (and a very minor one out of Milwaukee) until a regional authority was formed during the 1970s to assume funding and operation of commuter-rail services throughout Chicagoland.

FREIGHT INNOVATIONS on the Milwaukee Road included the 1964 introduction of the *XL Special* and *Thunderhawk*, priority transcontinental freight trains between Chicago and Tacoma, Washington. Milwaukee was also one of the pioneers in limited-crew, high-speed intermodal (container and truck trailers on flat cars) service, introducing *Sprint* train service between Chicago and the Twin Cities in 1978.

Unfortunately, innovations and the reduction of unprofitable passenger services were not enough to save the Milwaukee Road from big trouble. Here was a railroad that had a web of trackage all over a region of the Midwest that was already rife with rail lines of other carriers, principally C&NW but also Soo Line, Rock Island, Chicago Great Western (merged with C&NW in 1968), Illinois Central and Chicago, Burlington & Quincy (Burling-

Text continued on page 66

The Skytop parlor-observation cars of the Chicago-Twin Cities *Morning Hiawatha* and *Afternoon Hiawatha* stand side by side at Minneapolis on a frigid winter evening in 1969. These unique passenger cars, with their glass-roofed lounging area at one end of the car, were conceived by noted industrial designer, the late Brooks Stevens (who also designed the Studebaker and Excalibur automobiles and the 1950 Harley-Davidson). The cars were built by the Milwaukee Road at its Milwaukee Shops in 1952.—MIKE SCHAFER.

One of the most remote and lonely outposts on the Milwaukee Road had to be Avery, Idaho, deep in the Bitterroot Mountains. For through trains operating along the Pacific Extension, crews were changed at Avery on eastbound Tacoma-Chicago trains and electric locomotives added to take the trains over the mountains and beyond to Harlowton, Montana, the eastern end of the Rocky Mountain electrified zone. Conversely, westbound freights acquired electric locomotives at Harlowton and dropped them off at Avery while crews were changed. At Avery engine terminal during the wee hours of a September morning in 1971, two "box-cab" electric locomotive sets wait to assist the next train through town. These elderly "motors," as electric railroad locomotives are often called, were built by General Electric 1916 and had been in continuous service on the Milwaukee Road since that time. They would survive another three years, into 1974, when cash-starved Milwaukee Road, unable to afford upgrading the electrical-distribution system and the purchase new electric locomotives, abandoned all electric operations.—MIKE SCHAFER.

ton Northern as of March 1970). Further, the Milwaukee was the weakest of all the lines that stretched to the Pacific Northwest from the Midwest, and its Pacific Extension had become a huge drain on resources.

Finally, in 1977, the Chicago, Milwaukee, St. Paul & Pacific filed for bankruptcy and reorganization. The Milwaukee was not alone. A number of railroads throughout North America experienced difficult financial periods in the late 1960s and 1970s. Those in regions overbuilt with rail lines during the rail building boom years of the 19th and early 20th centuries were particularly hard hit.

Finally, in 1980, desperate times had called for desperate action: The Milwaukee Road began a widespread abandonment of all but its most prosperous "core" lines in an effort to conserve cash and drastically reduce operating expenses. It shed most of the Pacific Extension, its main line to Omaha west of the Mississippi River and numerous secondary main lines and branch lines, retrenching into a system radiating out of Chicago and Milwaukee to the Twin Cities, Duluth, Louisville, Kansas City, Green Bay, western Iowa and eastern South Dakota. The plan more or less worked, and Milwaukee Road once again became a viable (if greatly downsized) property—one that was now considerably more attractive to other buyers.

In 1985, most of the Milwaukee Road was purchased by one-time rival Soo Line Railroad, which today is operated by Canadian Pacific under the name "CP Rail Heavy Haul U.S." Gone is the long-familiar Milwaukee Road canted emblem and the sprinting Indian logo, both heralding a memorable tradition of speed and service.

LEFT: Milwaukee Road had many quaint branch lines throughout America's heartland, particularly in Wisconsin and Iowa. This local train is en route from Platteville, Wisconsin, at the end of a spur off the Mineral Point branch, to its home base at Janesville, Wisconsin, in 1971. There's not much business today—only two cars of aggregate from the quarries near Platteville; in fact, lack of business led to the Platteville line's demise shortly after this photo was recorded. If being picturesque could have paid bills, the Milwaukee Road would have been a wealthy railroad.—MIKE SCHAFER.

LEFT: A maroon-banded set of F-unit locomotives works the north yard at Davis Junction, Illinois, intersection of Milwaukee Road's Beloit (Wisconsin)-McNabb (Illinois) line and its Chicago-Council Bluffs main line.—JIM BOYD. BELOW: Premier trains of Milwaukee Road's Chicago-Council Bluffs main line were Union Pacific's transcontinental Streamliners and Domeliners, which in October 1955 were shifted from Chicago & North Western tracks to Milwaukee Road tracks between Chicago and Council Bluffs. On a fall afternoon in 1969, the combined *City of Portland/City of Denver* departs the tangle of Chicago behind two Milwaukee Road locomotives. By midnight, the train will be handed over to the UP at Omaha.—MIKE SCHAFER.

Chicago, Rock Island & Pacific

The story of the legendary Chicago, Rock Island & Pacific was one of both triumph and tragedy. Here was a company which endured almost 130 years, becoming a transportation institution in the Midwest and South Central U.S. Rock Island Lines even had a popular song devoted to it. Yet, fame did not ensure fortune, for the entire Rock Island died a pauper, closing down during the course of a wintery day in 1980.

The enterprise that became the Rock Island began modestly in the 1840s. The Rock Island & La Salle Railroad Company initially planned to connect Rock Island, Illinois, on the Mississippi River, with the state-sponsored Illinois & Michigan Canal at La Salle/Peru. The I&M Canal linked the Great Lakes at Chicago with Peru, the head of steamboat navigation on the Illinois River.

After surveying its prospects, however, the RI&LS decided it could earn larger profits if it extended the railroad to Chicago, thereby diverting passengers from the slower canal boats. The State of Illinois authorized the extension in February 1851, at which time the company was renamed the Chicago & Rock Island Railroad. Tracklaying began at Chicago early in 1852 and reached Joliet, 40 miles from Chicago, on October 8, of that year. Pulled by a steam locomotive dubbed *The Rocket*, the first train between those cities ran on October 10, 1852.

Things were hardly moribund at the other end of the railroad during this period. Also in 1852, C&RI affiliate Mississippi & Missouri Railroad began building between Davenport and Council Bluffs, Iowa, via Des Moines. Meanwhile the C&RI continued its march to the Mississippi from Joliet and by February 1854 was operating trains over the entire 181-mile route between its namesake cities. Connection between the C&RI and the M&M would be via a new bridge across the 1,400-foot Mississippi narrows that separated Rock Island from Davenport. The bridge—the first

major span over the Mississippi—was completed in 1856, replacing the ferry boats that had connected the railroads.

The new C&RI-M&M system enjoyed early commercial success. Settlers swarmed west along the Rock Island's direct route to the virgin lands of eastern Iowa, which began to yield grain that was shipped by rail to established markets farther east.

Completion of the M&M across Iowa became an urgent priority following the news of Union Pacific's commencement of construction west from Omaha in 1863. There would be great benefits in connecting the Rock Island system with that of the new UP. To expedite construction, the Chicago, Rock Island & Pacific Railroad was created on May 26, 1866, to acquire the C&RI and M&M and finance construction. The last rail in the line to Council Bluffs was spiked on May 11, 1869, one day after Union Pacific and Central Pacific had been bolted together at Promontory, Utah.

Rock Island's expansion during the 1870s was limited to various short branches and an ill-fated line to Leavenworth, Kansas. In 1879, the Rock Island and Chicago, Burlington & Quincy jointly purchased the Burlington, Cedar Rapids & Northern, a line between Burlington, Iowa, and Albert Lea, Minnesota (Rock Island would acquire full control in 1902). Later the same year, the Rock Island reached St. Joseph and Kansas City, Missouri, which greatly increased the railroad's business to and from the Southwest.

The 1880s saw greater expansion of the American railroad network than any other decade, and most of the other Western railroads indulged in frenzied track-laying. Initially, the Rock Island chose to stand pat, but by 1886 the company had become convinced that expansion was indeed necessary. The company organized the Chicago, Kansas & Nebraska Railway to build three major extensions, all of which opened in 1888: the South-

FACING PAGE: Operating on Union Pacific trackage rights, an eastbound Rock Island freights growls past the UP depot at Lawrence, Kansas. It's August 14, 1954, and Rock Island is six years out of its most recent bankruptcy, enjoying the fruits of the aggressive Farrington leadership. Farrington management totally dieselized the Rock Island by the end of that year and was in the process of revamping much of the road's physical property.—WALLACE W. ABBEY. FACING PAGE INSET: Rock Island's familiar herald still adorned the depot at Faribault, Minnesota, in 1984, even though the railroad had vanished four years earlier.—STEVE GLISCHINSKI. LEFT: A public timetable from 1944 touts the new fleet of *Rocket* streamliners.

ROCK ISLAND AT A GLANCE

Headquarters: Chicago, Illinois

Mileage:
1950: 7,579

Locomotives owned as of 1963:
Diesel: 539

Rolling stock owned as of 1963:
Freight cars: 26,690   Passenger: 646

Principal routes as of 1950:
Chicago-Omaha, Neb.
Omaha-Colorado Springs/Denver, Colo.
Davenport, Iowa-Tucumcari, N.M.
Bureau Junction-Peoria, Ill.
Minneapolis, Minn.-Kansas City, Mo.
Manly-Burlington, Iowa
Cedar Rapids (Vinton), Iowa-Sioux Falls, S. Dak.
Keokuk, Iowa-Bear Lake, S. Dak.
Tucumcari-Memphis, Tenn.
Herington, Kansas-Houston, Texas
Little Rock, Ark.-Eunice, La.
Kansas City-St. Louis, Mo.

Notable passenger trains (alphabetically):
Choctaw Rocket (Amarillo, Texas-Memphis)
Corn Belt Rocket (Chicago-Omaha)
Des Moines Rocket (Chicago-Des Moines, Iowa)
Golden State (Chicago-Los Angeles, jointly operated with Southern Pacific)
The *Imperial* (Chicago-Los Angeles)
Kansas City Rocket (Minneapolis-Kansas City)
Peoria Rockets (Chicago-Peoria)
Texas Rocket (Fort Worth-Houston, later Kansas City-Dallas)
Twin Star Rocket (Minneapolis-Houston)
Quad City Rocket (Chicago-Rock Island)
Rocky Mountain Rocket (Chicago-Colorado Springs/Denver)
Zephyr Rocket (Minneapolis-St. Louis, jointly operated with Chicago, Burlington & Quincy)

ABOVE: Long after they were history, Rock Island's earliest *Rocket* locomotives remain immortalized in an elaborate neon sign atop a warehouse in St. Paul in 1970.—WALLACE W. ABBEY. BELOW: CRI&P system map from a 1955 public timetable.

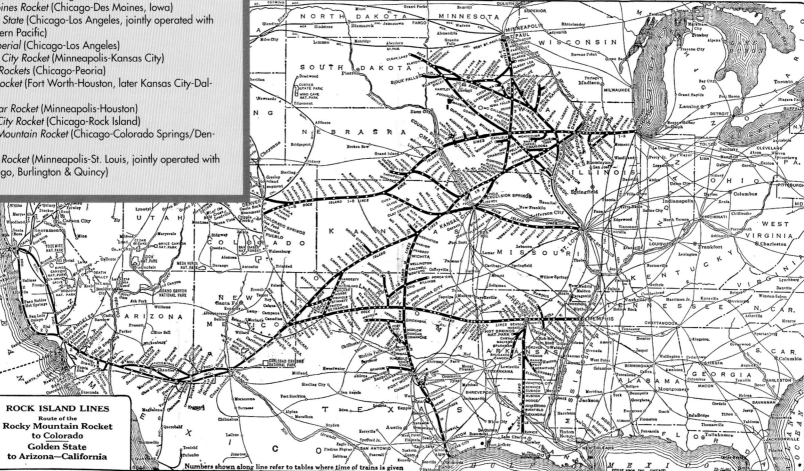

ROCK ISLAND LINES
Route of the
Rocky Mountain Rocket
to Colorado
Golden State
to Arizona—California

west Line from St. Joseph, Missouri, to Liberal, Kansas; the South Line from Herington (on the Southwest Line) into Indian Territory; and the West Line from Horton and McFarland, Kansas, to Colorado Springs, Colorado.

Despite the CK&N expansions, the Rock Island system remained fragmented, and between 1889 and 1893 the railroad had to close its various gaps through new construction, trackage rights or acquisition of lines from other railroads. Also in the 1890s, the South Line was extended to Fort Worth (1893) while several branches were built into unsettled regions of the I.T., which in 1907 became the State of Oklahoma.

In 1902 the Rock Island extended its Liberal line to Santa Rosa, New Mexico, meeting the rails of a Southern Pacific relative, the El Paso & North Eastern, which had built from its connection with the SP at El Paso. The Rock Island promptly arranged with EP&NE and SP to inaugurate a Chicago-California passenger train over this new transcontinental route. The *Golden State Limited* lent that appellation to the route, which would have enormous significance to the company in the coming years. The train itself survived until 1968.

Also in 1902, the Rock Island acquired the Choctaw, Oklahoma & Gulf Railroad between Memphis, Tennessee, and Amarillo, Texas. This line, which became known as the Rock's "Choctaw Route"—would become a link between the Southeast and Southwest once the gap between Amarillo and Tucumcari, New Mexico, was completed in 1910.

During the first decade of the 20th Century the Rock Island opened a number of new routes and lines, notably an extension from Kansas City to St. Louis (1904) and one from Fort Worth to the Gulf of Mexico at Galveston (1907). One of the last major pieces of the Rock Island puzzle was set in place in with the purchase of the St. Paul & Des Moines between Des Moines and Mason City, Iowa, in 1911 and the corresponding construction of a cutoff between Des Moines and the Davenport-Kansas City main line in 1913. This gave the Rock Island the shortest route between the Twin Cities and Kansas City—a line which would prove a valuable asset even after the railroad's 1980 abandonment.

During the first two decades of the 1900s, the Rock heavily modernized its system with automatic block signals, telephone dispatching and a major shop facility at Silvis, near Rock Island. In 1903, the company joined with Lake Shore & Michigan Southern (New York Central) in completing the new La Salle Street Station in Chicago.

In the dozen years between 1902 and 1914, the Rock Island grew from a 4,000-mile railroad to an 8,300-mile system serving a vastly-expanded territory. But growth and improvements did not result in financial success, for Rock Island entered receivership in 1915. Rising traffic levels returned the railroad to profitability by 1917, and in 1919—thanks largely to World War I—traffic reached record levels.

The cauldron of the Depression and the Dust Bowl, which consumed vast portions of the farmlands served by the Rock Island, resulted in enormous deficits for the railroad, forcing it to enter its second receivership in 1933. By May 1936, the railroad was in sorry shape. Annual deficits were at $10 to $15 million, passenger revenues had dropped by more than two- thirds, most of the rolling stock was obsolete, and property maintenance had been deferred. New Chief Executive Officer John D. Farrington, however, was deter-

BELOW: World War II is at end, but railroading appears to still be in full swing in this scene from July 1945 as double-headed 4-8-4's storm through Lawrence, Kansas, with a westbound freight.—WALLACE W. ABBEY.

ABOVE: By the time this view was recorded at Chicago's La Salle Street Station late in 1971, Rock Island's intercity passenger-train fleet had dwindled to two runs, both of which are awaiting their appointed departure times. At left in the distance is the two-car *Peoria Rocket* while at right is its somewhat healthier companion, the *Quad City Rocket*. With evening departure times less than 45 minutes apart, the two low-orbit *Rocket*s will follow one another to Bureau Junction, Illinois, where the Peoria train will head south along the Illinois River to its namesake and the *Quad City Rocket* will continue west to the Quad Cities of Davenport and Bettendorf, Iowa, and Rock Island and Moline, Illinois, all clustered on the Mississippi River.—ROGER PUTA, COLLECTION OF MEL FINZER.

mined to reverse the Rock Island's fortunes.

"Planned Progress" was what Farrington called his program for saving the railroad. Numerous improvement projects were brought to fruition: Heavier rail, new steel bridges, line changes to improve routes, extension of signalization and Centralized Traffic Control all brought the railroad's fixed plant closer to the standards maintained by wealthier lines in the West. Concurrently, the increased freight and passenger traffic resulting from World War II put the Rock Island back in the black in 1941.

The Farrington management was quick to adopt the cost-saving technology of the diesel-electric locomotive, despite the fact that the Rock Island had kept abreast of the latest developments in steam power. For example, in 1936 no other railroad could boast of such a

large fleet of Northern-type locomotives—4-8-4's. Nonetheless, Farrington brought the diesel and the streamlined passenger train to the Rock Island in 1937. General Motors' Electro-Motive Corporation built eleven standard switch engines and, to power the new stainless-steel *Rocket* streamliners, six new passenger diesels replete in stunning red, maroon and silver.

The original *Rocket*s, which provided fast and cheap coach-class service on intermediate-length day routes, were a cost-effective success which encouraged management to field streamliners in more lucrative travel markets. Thus in 1939 the Rock Island introduced the *Rocky Mountain Rocket* in direct competition with the overnight Chicago-Colorado streamliners of Burlington and Union Pacific-Chicago & North Western.

To its devotees, the postwar Rock Island was best known for its diverse diesel fleet and colorful commuter-train operations. LEFT: In 1956, General Motors built three futuristic LWT-12 locomotives (for "Lightweight, 1200 hp."), designed for two types of experimental lightweight passenger trains that ran in test service on the New York Central, Union Pacific, Pennsylvania Railroad and Rock Island. Rock wound up buying all three trains and their locomotives, and they spent their final years in unglorious Chicago suburban-train service. One of the trains, an *Aerotrain* set, arrives Chicago from Joliet, Illinois, on September 1, 1962, behind LWT-12 locomotive No. 2, which today resides in the National Railroad Museum in Green Bay, Wisconsin.—BOB JOHNSTON. BELOW: A relatively rare diesel type offered by GM's Electro-Motive Division after World War II was the BL-series (for "Branch Line") locomotive. Rock Island bought several, which it used on freight, passenger and commuter trains

The Rock Island emerged from bankruptcy on New Year's Day 1948. Farrington's improvement program continued unabated with millions spent on new hump-type classification yards, line relocations and more new rolling stock and diesels, the latter permitting the railroad to retire its last steam locomotives in 1954.

Unfortunately, even the new and improved Rock Island could not prevent the company's old problems from resurfacing. The pressure of stronger railroad competitors like Santa Fe and Union Pacific, along with strengthening motor-carrier competition and the continued decline of rural areas and small towns in middle America, amplified the weaknesses of the Rock Island's crazy-quilt route structure.

New management in 1956 responded to declining revenues and increasing costs by reducing surplus track and slashing passenger train miles—moves that were but stopgap efforts. Interestingly, and in hopes of reducing operating costs and wooing back passengers, the railroad experimented (unsuccessfully) with radical new passenger-train concepts in the late 1950s, purchasing the ultra-lightweight *Jet Rocket* and two *Aerotrains*.

Union Pacific, which had become solidly profitable with the growth of the West, was particularly interested in the Rock Island, which would have given UP direct access to Eastern gateways. In September 1964, UP filed to merge with Rock Island. For a multitude of reasons, it turned out to be one of the most-complex and agonizing merger proposals

alike. BL2 No. 429 pulls a train of "Al Capone" suburban cars into Englewood, Illinois, in July 1961. The round-roof, open-window commuter cars dated from the Roarin' Twenties, and they served commuters well into the 1970s.—DAN POPE COLLECTION.

ABOVE: Rock Island's St. Louis-Kansas City line never seemed to realize its full potential, considering it connected Missouri's two largest cities. What the line lacked in business, it more than made up in terms of scenery, as evidenced by the passing of the daily local westbound over the Gasconade River in July 1974. Following Rock's 1980 demise, the line was transferred to the St. Louis Southwestern Railway (Cotton Belt).—TERRY NORTON.

ever administered by the Interstate Commerce Commission.

During the interminable proceedings, the Rock Island slipped into the red in 1965. The officers kept the company going by deferring maintenance on the fixed plant, which had become a laughingstock by the early 1970s. Freight customers responded by rerouting their shipments, and what little passenger service remained was cut back to intrastate runs in Illinois by 1970.

Finally, in November 1974, the ICC allowed that UP could merge with the Rock Island—on a number of contingencies that would have resulted in many additional years of legal wrangling. UP promptly announced "thanks but no thanks," stunning the industry and leaving the ICC with egg on its face.

Bereft of its Omaha-based suitor and losing traffic rapidly due to its broken-down tracks and poor service, the Rock Island hired a new, go-for-broke management led by brash John

LEFT: In the 1960's, Rock Island provided the only direct rail link between Chicago and Illinois' then-second-largest city, Peoria. As the 1950s dawned, travelers could chose from eight Chicago-Peoria trains, four in each direction. By the summer of 1967, when this photo was taken at Rock Island's riverfront depot in downtown Peoria, service had been cut in half. The homely nose of diesel 621—a lone survivor of four DL-series Alco passenger diesels purchased by Rock Island during the World War II years—leads the morning *Peoria Rocket* on this sunny day. *Rocket*s, of course, no longer call at Peoria, but the depot today serves as a restaurant.—JIM BOYD.

BELOW: A daily ritual at Limon, Colorado, where Rock Island's Colorado Springs line crossed Union Pacific's Denver-Kansas City line, was the combining of the Denver and Springs sections of the *Rocky Mountain Rocket*. In this 1956 view looking north, the Denver section is about to swing east off the UP (on which CRI&P had trackage rights Denver-Limon). At left, minus its locomotive, which has uncoupled and pulled away, is the Colorado Springs section. The two sections will be switched into one train for the overnight journey to Chicago.—WALLACE W. ABBEY.

ABOVE: Wearing the Rock Island's eye-catching "barber shop pole" scheme, an Alco freight diesel and an EMD "Geep" (GP7 model) head up an eastbound freight at Topeka, Kansas, on November 6, 1955. By this time, Rock Island had also applied the "Rocket" moniker to its freight service (note the partially peeled "*Rocket* Freight" emblem on the lead locomotive).—WILLIAM A. GIBSON SR. Freight-related ads of the period (LEFT) advised potential customers to "Ship it Rock Island" and that the "Rock Island States of America" were directly served by "now famous *Rocket* Freights."

Ingram, late of the Federal Railroad Administration, in 1975. But it was too late. On March 17, 1975, the Rock Island entered its third, and last, bankruptcy.

Ingram and bankruptcy trustee William Gibbons plunged ahead with one more effort to save "The Rock." The railroad reduced freight train frequency, increased tonnage and cut yard engine jobs. The last of the passenger trains, the *Peoria Rocket* and the *Quad City Rocket* were discontinued at the end of 1978 (Rock Island had been too broke to join Amtrak in 1971 and was thus obligated by law to continue its passenger service). A modest upgrading of the main line across Illinois took place, and the railroad also acquired 80 new

The time to say
"Ship it Rock Island"
is when you have freight going to or from

Arkansas
Colorado
Illinois
Iowa
Kansas
Louisiana
Minnesota
Missouri
Nebraska
New Mexico
Oklahoma
South Dakota
Tennessee
Texas

These are the Rock Island States of America, directly served by this railroad with its modern facilities and the now famous ROCKET FREIGHTS. For shipments to foreign lands use the gulf ports of Houston, Texas City and Galveston.

For specific freight information consult any Rock Island representative.

Rock Island

ROCK ISLAND LINES *The Road of Planned Progress*

diesel locomotives. All this was accompanied by a new image: a modernistic blue-and-white "The Rock" scheme, which appeared on so many cars, locomotives and buildings that the railroad seemed to be trying to paint its way out of insolvency.

Rock Island's problems, though, ran far too deep to be painted over. Early in 1979, a cash crunch caused the carrier to embargo two of its weakest lines. When management refused to give in to labor's demands for higher pay, the unions struck the Rock Island. Unable to move traffic, the Rock could not generate cash to pay operating expenses, sealing its doom.

The ICC directed several railroads to take over the prostrate Rock Island's operations at the federal government's expense on Sept. 26, 1979. Late on the afternoon of Jan. 25, 1980, Judge McGarr ordered trustee Gibbons to cease operations and liquidate the property.

Most of Rock Island's strategic arteries remain in use today but are owned by surviving railroads (notably Union Pacific and Southern Pacific) and new companies such as Iowa Interstate. So, there is consolation in knowing that trains still ply the most-historic Rock route: that of the old Chicago & Rock Island between Chicago and Rock Island.

BELOW: In the early 1850s, the infant Chicago & Rock Island Railroad built west from Chicago along the Illinois & Michigan Canal. Completion of the railroad pretty much doomed canal business—the irony of which is that the I&M ended up outliving the Rock Island! For years moribund, the I&M Canal gained recognition as a national historic landmark and underwent restoration in the 1960s and 1970s. In the spring of 1975, a Chicago-bound Rock Island freight skirts the canal (and the Illinois River beyond) east of La Salle. The silver bridge in the distance carries Illinois Central's original north-south "charter line" across the Illinois River.—Tom Post.

ABOVE: The Twin Cities are is living up to their snowy reputation on a December evening in 1964 as Rock Island train No. 15, just in from nearby Minneapolis, loads passengers and mail at St. Paul Union Depot. Nameless No. 15 was an overnight Minneapolis-Kansas City train comprised largely of mail and express cars. A couple of reclining-seat coaches and a sleeping car were sufficient for the few passengers headed south this evening toward hopefully warmer climes. Leading the train is an early Electro-Motive passenger diesel, a model E3A built prior to World War II. One of Rock Island's unusual BL2 diesels trails.—RON LUNDSTROM.

ABOVE: In the late 1970s, Rock Island made one last valiant attempt to make a comeback, going so far as to paint equipment in a completely new blue-and-white scheme and officially adopt its recently acquired nickname, "The Rock", as part of a new, aggressive image. Wearing the new colors, three locomotives drift into Strasburg, Colorado, with a Denver-bound freight on February 27, 1980. The railroad had already folded when this scene along Union Pacific's Kansas City–Denver line (on which Rock Island had trackage rights west of Limon), and operations were being handled by other railroads, often still using Rock Island equipment.—STEVE PATTERSON. RIGHT: A scrapyard scene at Silvis, Illinois, in 1981 vividly portrayed the ignominious end to one of America's most legendary railroads.—STEVE SMEDLEY.

MAIN LINE THRU THE ROCKIES

Denver & Rio Grande Western

80 CLASSIC AMERICAN RAILROADS

Entrenched in the mystique of Colorado, the Rio Grande Railroad has long been revered by students of railroading. Here is a railroad that passes through spectacular scenery, has a colorful history involving charismatic narrow-gauge railroading in Colorado's silver era, and features one of the seven wonders of American railroad engineering: the Moffat Tunnel.

In the pioneer days, lines of emigration to the great American West only skirted Colorado, with the Santa Fe trail veering southwest and the Oregon Trail northwest. The imposing Colorado Rockies were just too much of a barrier to westward expansion in Colorado Territory per se early in the 19th Century. The discovery of gold in the Front Range of the Rockies changed all that, and the resulting boom fostered Denver City at the base of the Rockies.

As people began settling along the Front Range, railroads soon followed, including Union Pacific affiliates Denver Pacific and Kansas Pacific, linking Denver with Kansas City and Cheyenne. Eventually Denver became prosperous enough to push for railroad expansion west and south from the city, and one of the earliest endeavors serving this goal was the Denver & Rio Grande Railway, chartered in 1870.

A narrow-gauge railroad, the D&RG was headed south toward El Paso, Texas, with the intention of paralleling its namesake river from southern Colorado to Mexico. It planned to do this by building southward along the face of the Rockies to Pueblo and then turning west to squeeze through the awesomely narrow and deep Royal Gorge of the Arkansas River to reach the Rio Grande. After it had reached Pueblo in 1872, the railroad altered its sights to using Raton Pass in northern New Mexico instead—but so did the approaching Santa Fe, which was planning to build west over Raton and through the Royal Gorge. The two railroads went to war, almost literally, in 1878. The result? Santa

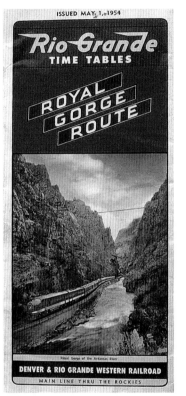

ISSUED MAY 1, 1954

Rio Grande
TIME TABLES

ROYAL GORGE ROUTE

Royal Gorge of the Arkansas River

DENVER & RIO GRANDE WESTERN RAILROAD
MAIN LINE THRU THE ROCKIES

Fe got Raton and Rio Grande got the Gorge.

By 1880, railroad magnate and financier Jay Gould owned a large interest in D&RG, and its direction took a different turn, dropping its plans to head to Mexico. By this time D&RG had already built through the Royal Gorge to Salida and Leadville to serve areas rich with timber, coal, silver, and gold, and it was also building lines through the San Juan Range to such legendary locales as Durango and Silverton, Colorado, and Santa Fe, New Mexico. D&RG's new goal was to extend one of its lines over the Continental Divide to Salt Lake City and Ogden, Utah. This plan was accomplished through the formation of another narrow-gauge carrier, the Denver & Rio Grande Western Railway (later renamed Rio Grande Western). The D&RGW was leased to the D&RG to build from Salt Lake City east to Green River, Utah, where in 1883 it met the D&RG, which had been building west from Salida through Gunnison, Colorado.

The use of three-foot-gauge track rather than the standard gauge of four feet, eight and a half inches saved on construction costs and made it easier for railroads to penetrate the harrowing confines of the Rockies. Although narrow-gauge construction worked for the long term on many of D&RG's mineral branches, it thwarted through traffic interchange with standard-gauge railroads. For this reason, D&RG began standard-gauging its Denver-Pueblo-Leadville route early in the 1880s.

In the late 1880s, D&RG affiliates began building a standard-gauge line toward Salt Lake City, extending from Leadville westward over Tennessee Pass—at the time the highest point on a standard-gauge railroad in America—and through Glenwood Canyon. In 1890 this line reached the earlier RGW-D&RG through route at what became Grand Junction, Colorado. The opening of the newer through route, which included the standard-gauging of the old RGW, changed everything.

FACING PAGE: Denver & Rio Grande Western probably boasted more spectacular scenery per mile than any other American railroad. Westbound train No. 17, the Denver-Salt Lake City *Rio Grande Zephyr*, gives its passengers a grand dose of some of that scenery as the train snakes through South Boulder Canyon near Pinecliff, Colorado, on June 30, 1979, during the 50-mile climb out of the Mile High City to Moffat Tunnel.—JOE McMILLAN. FACING PAGE INSET: The railroad's neon sign atop the Salt Lake City depot is a landmark that can be seen for blocks.—MIKE SCHAFER. LEFT: A D&RGW public timetable from 1954 featured a colorized photo of the Vista-Dome *Royal Gorge* in its namesake canyon.

ABOVE: Rio Grande was a dual-personality railroad. Its stainless-steel transcon passenger train, the *California Zephyr,* and its modern diesel power were a contrast to the railroad's narrow-gauge routes in southern Colorado and northern New Mexico. Here, time had stopped. Steam still ruled the three-foot-gauge lines that D&RGW kept operating well after World War II to such fabled places as Durango and Silverton, Colorado, and Chama, New Mexico. In 1956, engine 480 pauses for water at the Chama tank during a freight run. This was not a staged operation for tourists; this was how Rio Grande still operated its narrow-gauge lines!—RAILROAD AVENUE ENTERPRISES.

The Rio Grande was now an important link in the transcontinental rail system, and by the early 1890s was hosting through passenger trains between Denver and California.

RGW was merged into D&RG in 1908; meanwhile, D&RG was financing the construction of the Western Pacific between Salt Lake City and Oakland (San Francisco). The WP was completed in 1909 and became Rio Grande's principal connection to the West Coast. The following year Denver-Oakland through passenger service began. In 1915, a joint Missouri Pacific-D&RG-WP deluxe train, the *Scenic Limited,* was inaugurated between St. Louis and Oakland via Pueblo and the Royal Gorge. Unfortunately, the WP went bankrupt and took the D&RG with it. D&RG emerged from the bankruptcy in 1921 as the Denver & Rio Grande Western Railroad

Our story now returns to Denver, which was still pushing for a more-direct route to

Salt Lake City. Behind what would become the key for such a route was David Moffat, one-time D&RG president and prominent Denver businessman. Since almost the turn of the century, Moffat's Denver, Northwestern & Pacific Railroad had been building a line that was headed ultimately for Salt Lake.

The line crossed the Continental Divide northwest of Denver at Rollins Pass—elevation 11,680 feet—via what at least one historian has described as a "fantasy of steel"—a steep, tortuous, twisting climb over the spine of the Divide. It took almost 25 miles of zig-zag trackage to connect two points on either side of the crest that in reality were less than eight miles apart if connected by a tunnel. A raft of helper locomotives stood by to escort trains over the 4 percent grade of the "Giant's Ladder." In mainline railroading, 2 percent grades are considered very steep.

The DN&P, later renamed Denver & Salt

ABOVE: Yard duties completed for the time being, two D&RGW switchers idle away the evening hours at Rio Grande's North Yard in Denver in April 1971 while a set of road diesels (background) receive sand (for wheel traction) and fuel for their next mountain-climbing assignment.—MIKE SCHAFER.

RIO GRANDE AT A GLANCE

Headquarters: Denver, Colorado

Mileage
1950: 2,413
1995: 2,238 including trackage rights routes

Locomotives owned as of 1963:
Steam: 22   Diesel: 257

Rolling stock owned as of 1963:
Freight cars: 12,610   Passenger: 96

Principal lines as of 1950:
Denver-Bond, Colo.-Salt Lake City, Utah
Denver-Pueblo-Dotsero, Colo.
Pueblo-Trinidad, Colo.
Walsenburg-Alamosa, Colo.
Alamosa-Durango, Colo.
Salida-Gunnison, Colo.
Mears Junction-Alamosa
Alamosa-Creede, Colo.
Bond-Craig, Colo.
Grand Junction-Ouray, Colo.
Thistle-Marysvale, Utah
Salt Lake City-Ogden, Utah

Notable passenger trains (alphabetically):
California Zephyr (Chicago-Oakland, joint with Burlington and Western Pacific)
Colorado Eagle (St. Louis-Pueblo-Denver, joint with Missouri Pacific)
Exposition Flyer (Chicago-Oakland, joint with Burlington and Western Pacific, replaced by *California Zephyr* in 1949)
Mountaineer (Denver-Montrose, Colo., via Moffat Tunnel)
Panoramic (Denver-Ogden)
Prospector (Denver-Salt Lake City)
Rio Grande Zephyr (Denver-Ogden [later cut back to Salt Lake City], replaced *California Zephyr* 1970-1983)
Royal Gorge (Denver-Pueblo-Ogden)
San Juan (Alamosa-Durango, Colo.)
The *Silverton* (Durango-Silverton, Colo.)
The *Yampa Valley* (Denver-Craig)

MAP OF THE
DENVER & RIO GRANDE WESTERN RAILROAD
AND CONNECTIONS

SINGLE TRACK..........
DOUBLE TRACK..........

ABOVE: Rio Grande's route south from Denver to Pueblo is a shared-trackage arrangement with Burlington Northern Santa Fe known as the "Joint Line." The multi-track line to this day is a busy artery for rail traffic, much of it in the form of unit coal trains. Three Rio Grande Electro-Motive SD45-2 locomotives have their work cut out for them as they lug a coal train northward at Palmer Lake, Colorado, on August 25, 1986.—STEVE PATTERSON.

Lake (and long referred to as the "Moffat Road" for its founder), never reached Salt Lake City, though, much Utah. Instead, construction had ended in coal country at Craig, Colorado, in 1913. In 1922, the City of Denver passed a bill to fund construction of a tunnel under James Peak. The $18 million 6.1-mile Moffat Tunnel opened in 1928, ending operations on the 23-mile mountain-climbing crawl over Rollins Pass. What had taken trains hours to negotiate now took about 15 minutes.

The Moffat Tunnel strengthened the D&SL's conviction to establish a through route to Salt Lake City. Thanks to the now-powerful D&RGW, this happened in 1934 with the opening of the 40-mile Dotsero Cutoff between Orestod, on the D&SL, and Dotsero on the D&RGW's Denver-Pueblo-Salt Lake main line. Using trackage rights on the D&SL between Denver and Orestod, D&RGW's Denver-Salt Lake route had become 175 miles shorter. Denver's long-time dream was reality.

Although D&RGW immediately began routing freight and passenger trains over the new route, including the new *Panoramic*, the impoverished D&SL was in need of rebuilding to make it fit for heavier locomotives and more

traffic. Through D&RGW, this rebuild was accomplished, culminating with the 1939 inauguration of the new Burlington-Rio Grande-Western Pacific *Exposition Flyer* between Chicago and Oakland via the Moffat Tunnel. In 1941, the overnight Denver-Salt Lake City *Prospector* went into service. Denver-Pueblo-Ogden passenger service continued with a train aptly named the *Royal Gorge*.

In 1947, the D&SL was merged into the D&RGW. In 1949, one of the most famous passenger trains in U.S. history was launched by CB&Q-D&RGW-WP. The Vista-Dome *California Zephyr* replaced the *Exposition Flyer* on the Chicago-Oakland run, its schedule purposely arranged to traverse the super-scenic Denver-Salt Lake route in daylight. The stainless-steel train was an instant hit.

Like most other railroads of the postwar era, dieselization became a priority for D&RGW, but interestingly the railroad did not fully dieselize until 1979. Emerging from its second bankruptcy in 1947, D&RGW became modern and dynamic in the postwar years, but it still harbored some anachronisms: Steam-powered narrow-gauge trains still poked their way through the ranges of southern Colorado and northern New Mexico with freight and passengers. Although the famed *San Juan* narrow-gauge passenger run vanished from the timetables in 1951, tourists began riding an obscure, tri-weekly mixed (freight and passenger) train named the *Silverton* between Durango and Silverton—so much so that by 1964 the railroad had to build new cars for the run and increase service!

In 1967 D&RGW ceased all narrow-gauge operations outside the Silverton route. Much of the narrow-gauge network was abandoned, and in 1979 the whole Silverton line—train, locomotives and all—was sold to an individual. The line between Chama, New Mexico, and Antonito, Colorado, met a similar good fate, and both narrow-gauge lines still run.

FOLLOWING THE 1934 OPENING of the Dotsero Cutoff, Rio Grande became a strategic link in east-west traffic. Freight traffic out of the Ogden and Salt Lake City gateways could go either via the Royal Gorge route or the Moffat Tunnel route. Royal Gorge traffic largely was destined to and from the Missouri Pacific, Santa Fe, and Colorado & Southern (Burlington) at Pueblo while traffic through the Moffat Tunnel was destined to Denver proper or beyond on the Burlington, Union Pacific, or Rock Island. Rio Grande also ran considerable traffic originating at Denver south to Pueblo and Trinidad, Colorado. Meanwhile, the Craig branch grew in importance during the 1970s and 1980s as clean-burning Western coal became a highly sought commodity.

The original *California Zephyr* was dropped in 1970 and replaced by a Chicago-Ogden train

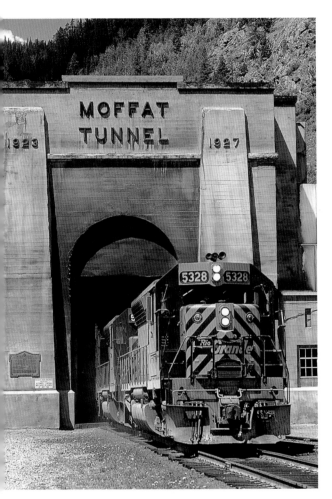

ABOVE: A Denver-bound freight emerges from the fortress-like facade of Moffat Tunnel's east portal in August 1971.—TOM BROWN. RIGHT: For 21 years the celebrated Vista-Dome *California Zephyr*—pride of the Burlington, Rio Grande and Western Pacific—showed travelers what scenery and train travel was all about. The westbound *CZ* is negotiating South Boulder Canyon near Wonder View, Colorado, in July 1969. The train was discontinued in 1970 and replaced by the *Rio Grande Zephyr*—which in turn was replaced by a revived *California Zephyr* operated by Amtrak.—MIKE SCHAFER.

operated by Burlington and Rio Grande; on the latter it was known as the *Rio Grande Zephyr*. D&RGW was one of the few railroads eligible to join Amtrak in 1971 which opted not to do so, and thus was obligated to continue operating the *Rio Grande Zephyr*. In an interesting reversal of events, Amtrak reincarnated its own version of the *California Zephyr* in 1983, operating it via the Rio Grande, which then was permitted to drop the *RGZ*.

In a mid-1980s move that essentially doubled the width of the railroad, D&RGW extended its operations east from Pueblo over 620 miles to Kansas City via a special trackage-rights agreement with Missouri Pacific.

The Rio Grande of the 1990s is hardly recognizable. In 1988, Rio Grande Industries, parent company of D&RGW, purchased the sprawling Southern Pacific Railroad, which initially presented a sort of tail-wagging-the-dog scenario. Eventually, though, SP influence altered the Rio Grande operationally and cosmetically. D&RGW enjoyed an increase in through traffic off SP routes since Rio Grande provided a short cut for SP traffic originating in Northern California and Oregon and des-

ABOVE: A single Alco PA passenger diesel is more than ample motive power for train 9, the *Yampa Valley*, departing Denver in June 1967. Westbound, the *Yampa Valley* tagged about 30 minutes behind its big sister, the *California Zephyr*, up to and through Moffat Tunnel. At Bond, Colorado, the *CZ* headed down the Dotsero Cutoff while the *Yampa Valley* continued up the old Denver & Salt Lake main line to its terminus at Craig, Colorado.—AL SCHULTZ. RIGHT: For 13 years, from 1970 to 1983, the *Rio Grande Zephyr* served as an ersatz *California Zephyr* on the Denver-Salt Lake City segment of the late, lamented *CZ*'s transcon route. Rio Grande operated its *RGZ* using some of the same cars used on the original *CZ* (Burlington, Rio Grande and WP all owned and pooled sets of *CZ* cars when that train was still running). The signature car of both the *CZ* and its *RGZ* descendant was the Vista-Dome observation lounge-sleeper, here lit up by a dozen flash units as the eastbound RGZ descends the Front Range of the Rockies on the final approach to Denver, whose city lights shimmer some 20 miles distant.—MIKE SCHAFER/MEL PATRICK.

tined for central U.S. gateways like Chicago, Kansas City, and St. Louis. Even though D&RGW technically remains a separate railroad, its corporate identity was a casualty of the takeover. D&RGW black-and-orange diesels have given way to SP's long-familiar gray and red, although SP's updated lettering scheme has adopted Rio Grande's distinctive speed-line lettering.

The face of Rio Grande may change again as the sun sets on the 20th Century and Western U.S. railroads vie for new alliances—notably a 1995 proposal for SP and UP to merge. For the time being, one thing remains constant as the 1990s wind down: The famed *California Zephyr* still traverses Glenwood Canyon, Moffat Tunnel and the Big Ten Loops, just as it did nearly a half century earlier. The train is often sold out, proving that the best way West is "Through the Rockies . . . Not Around Them" (as early Rio Grande travel brochures boldly proclaimed). And the best way to do that is by train over the Denver & Rio Grande Western.

ABOVE: A trio of Electro-Motive diesels led by a classic GP30 model sweep through the high desert country of eastern Utah near Thompson with westbound merchandise. The westbound *California Zephyr* is probably not too far behind the freight on this crystal clear November afternoon in 1969.— JOE MCMILLAN.

GREAT FOR TRAVEL, GREAT FOR FREIGHT

Great Northern

The Great Northern Railway proved that even a single person can have a profound effect on a large railroad—and even a whole region of the United States. That person was James J. Hill, the "Empire Builder."

Though now regarded as one of the most famous of railroad magnates that shaped American railroading, Hill initially established his wealth through a steamboat company he formed. Born in 1838, Hill did not get into the railroad business until 1878 when he bought into the fledgling St. Paul & Pacific—the first railroad to operate a train in Minnesota. The StP&P linked St. Paul to the U.S.-Canadian border at St. Vincent, Minnesota, and handled considerable traffic destined to and from Winnipeg, Manitoba.

The StP&P was purchased in 1879 by the St. Paul, Minneapolis & Manitoba, which had been formed by Hill. Under that name, the railroad began building westward, reaching Great Falls, Montana, in 1887 where another Hill concern, the Montana Central, would build to Butte, in the southwest corner of the state.

In 1889, Hill formed yet another railroad, the Great Northern Railway, which leased and eventually purchased the "Manitoba." The Great Northern Railway Company became Hill's vehicle for expanding west from Havre, Montana, to the Pacific. The trick was getting over the Rocky Mountains in a cost-effective manner and with a routing that kept relatively easy grades. This task was accomplished by engineer John F. Stevens, who discovered an obscure pass, Marias, in what is today Glacier National Park. In fact, GN and Hill's son Louis would play a critical role in the development of this park. For many years, GN offered the only means of getting into the park and until 1960 owned hotel properties in the park.

Once past the Rockies, the GN faced another, more-foreboding barrier: Washington's

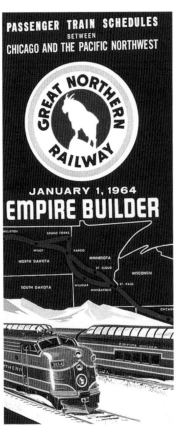

Cascade Range. Here as well, Stevens found a pass (which to this day bears his name) through the Cascades which would lead the railroad to a route down the west slopes to Puget Sound. In 1893, GN opened all the way to Seattle. In 1900, the 2.63-mile Cascade Tunnel opened under the ridge of the Cascade summit, eliminating a brutal, exposed climb over the pinnacle of the range that required "switchbacks" and large segments of trestlework. The tunnel and its trackage including approaches were electrified in 1909, requiring all trains to change from steam to electric locomotives and vice versa for the trip through the tunnel.

Despite his newfound success as a railroad man, Hill still had some marine blood in him. Once his GN made it to the Pacific coast, Hill formed the Great Northern Steamship Company, which in effect stretched the GN to the Orient. His son Louis assumed chief stewardship of the GN in 1912, and in 1916 James J. Hill died at the age of 77.

The Great Northern rode out the turbulence of the first half of the 20th Century remarkably well, in part thanks to new CEO Ralph Budd, who assumed GN leadership in 1919. GN roared on during the Roarin' Twenties, guided by Budd, whose name became synonymous with GN's modernization and upgrading during that period. Budd heavily modernized the GN steam-locomotive fleet with new or rebuilt engines, including a series of massive articulated (two separate sets of drivers, to carry a longer boiler) steam locomotives for pulling trains over the mountains.

The Budd reign culminated in 1929 with two major events: First, a new and longer Cascade Tunnel opened, replacing the original tunnel, and the electrification of the old tunnel was relocated through the new. Nearly 8 miles long, the new bore and its new approaches eliminated several more severe grades. Second, the "incomparable" *Empire*

FACING PAGE: As a railroad with lofty goals and a solid record of achievement, Great Northern was among the most respected carriers in the Pacific Northwest and upper Midwest. Symbolic, perhaps, of GN's progressiveness is Cascade Tunnel, out of which an eastbound freight emerges. The original Cascade Tunnel opened in 1900. Not satisfied with this achievement, GN opened a longer, better Cascade Tunnel in 1929, shown here on May 1, 1958.—MONTY POWELL. FACING PAGE INSET: There was little doubt as to which railroad owned this boxcar, photographed fresh out of the shops in 1956.—HOMER G. BENTON. LEFT: The GN passenger timetable from January 1964 featured the Great Dome *Empire Builder* on the cover.

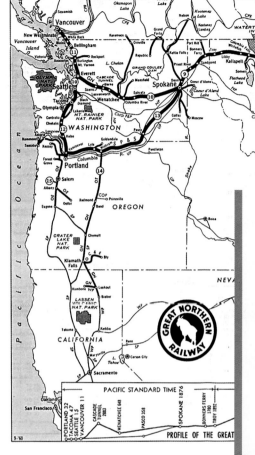

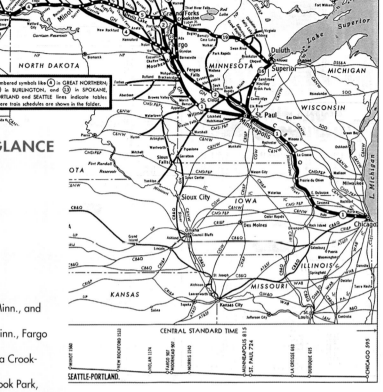

GREAT NORTHERN AT A GLANCE

Headquarters: St. Paul, Minnesota

Mileage
1950: 8,220

Locomotives owned as of 1963:
Diesel: 642

Rolling stock owned as of 1963:
Freight cars: 39,055   Passenger: 579

Principal routes as of 1950:

St. Paul, Minn.-Seattle, Wash. via Willmar, Minn., and New Rockford, N. Dak.

Minneapolis-Minot, N. Dak. via St. Cloud, Minn., Fargo and Grand Forks, N. Dak.

Superior, Wis./Duluth, Minn.-Grand Forks via Crookston, Minn.

Minneapolis/St. Paul-Duluth/Superior via Brook Park, Minn.

Barnesville, Minn.-Winnipeg, Man., via Ada and Crookston, Minn.

Portland, Ore.-Vancouver, B.C. via Seattle, Wash. (trackage rights on Northern Pacific Portland-Seattle)

Willmar-Sioux Falls, S. Dak./Sioux City, Iowa

Havre-Great Falls-Helena-Butte, Mont.

Shelby-Great Falls-Billings, Mont.

Bend, Ore.-Bieber, Calif., via Klamath Falls, Ore.

Notable passenger trains (alphabetically):

Badger (St. Paul-Minneapolis-Superior-Duluth)
Cascadian (Seattle-Spokane, Wash.)
Dakotan (St. Paul-Minneapolis-Williston, N. Dak.)
Empire Builder (Chicago-Seattle/Portland, operated jointly with Chicago, Burlington & Quincy and Spokane, Portland & Seattle)
Gopher (St. Paul-Minneapolis-Superior-Duluth)
International (Seattle-Vancouver, B.C.)
Oriental Limited (Chicago-Seattle/Portland, operated jointly with Chicago, Burlington & Quincy and Spokane, Portland & Seattle)
Red River (St. Paul-Minneapolis-Grand Forks, N. Dak.)
Western Star (Chicago-Seattle/Portland, operated jointly with Chicago, Burlington & Quincy and Spokane, Portland & Seattle)
Winnipeg Limited (St. Paul-Minneapolis-Winnipeg)

ABOVE: A Great Northern map from a 1964 passenger timetable made the railroad seem more extensive than it really was by showing Burlington's Twin Cities-Chicago line and Spokane, Portland & Seattle's Spokane-Portland route as though they were part of GN's mainline network. In a sense they were, for Burlington and SP&S were key operators of the *Empire Builder* and *Western Star* streamliners.

Builder was launched. Named for James J. Hill, the *Builder* became GN's star train between Chicago, Seattle and Portland. Chicago, Burlington & Quincy (Burlington Route), which relayed the *Builder* (and considerable GN freight traffic) between St. Paul and Chicago, participated in the train's operation through joint ownership of *Builder* rolling stock. In a like manner, the Spokane, Portland & Seattle Railway, another Hill concern, handled the *Builder*'s Portland section west of Spokane.

It was also during the 1910s that GN adopted a corporate logo featuring a mountain goat, indigenous to the Montana Rockies. With "Rocky" as its centerpiece, GN's emblem became one of the most widely recognized railroad logos of all time, and variations of the goat logo remained in use until GN's 1970 merger into Burlington Northern.

GN sampled diesel power in 1937, purchas-

LEFT: GN's Mikados (2-8-2's) were a break from tradition: As freight engines on most other railroads, "Mikes" normally had relatively small driving wheels—about 63 inches in diameter—better for lugging, but at moderate speeds. GN's Class O-8 2-8-2's had 69-inch driving wheels for high-speed running in the vast, relatively level prairies of Minnesota and eastern Montana. The 3383 is at Minneapolis in 1956.
BELOW: As with nearly every other U.S. railroad, diesels doomed steam on the GN, but at the same time they added a splash of color to operations. This pristine Electro-Motive F7A freight diesel at the roundhouse of GN's Interbay engine facility in Seattle displays the railroad's striking color scheme—certainly a top contender for the Top Ten Greatest Railroad Paint Schemes Ever Created. Date: August 28, 1956.—STEVE HAYWORTH.

GN founder James J. Hill was known as the "Empire Builder," so it was only natural that the railroad's signature train, launched in 1929, would carry that name. Initially a deluxe steam-powered heavyweight train, the *Empire Builder* became a streamliner in 1947. With its new Electro-Motive E7A passenger diesels and Pullman-Standard rolling stock, the 1947 *Builder* poses in northwestern Montana for its portrait. (A close look at the photo will reveal a freight in the distance patiently waiting for the company photographer to forever capture the newly born streamliner on film.) If a person were to stand at this location in 1996, he or she could still watch the *Empire Builder* pass by, albeit as a double-deck stainless-steel Amtrak train.—COLLECTION OF MIKE SCHAFER.

ing two 900-h.p. switching locomotives from General Motors' Electro-Motive Corporation. Satisfied that diesels were more than just curios, GN ordered another dozen switchers. Then in 1940, EMC demonstrated streamlined freight diesels on the GN, convincing the railroad that diesel power was indeed the way of the future for all train operations. Just as World War II erupted, delivery began on the first of 96 of these road diesels, the first to wear GN's handsome dark green, orange, and yellow paint scheme—livery considered by many rail historians to be to be one of the all-time classic railroad paint schemes.

Great Northern emerged from the war with its attention fully focused on the future. Dieselization resumed at full bore (the federal

government had limited diesel purchases during the war), and plans for revamping a war-weary passenger train fleet were given high priority. The first result of the latter project was the 1947 introduction of the new, diesel-powered streamlined *Empire Builder*—one of the first postwar streamliners to burnish American rails.

In its streamlined incarnation, the newly equipped *Builder* was a hit, earning several million dollars for GN and co-operator Burlington (which owned some of new streamlined equipment) during its first year in service. Bolstered by this success, GN ordered more streamlined cars and locomotives in 1949, and by the end of 1951 most of its principal trains had been re-equipped—including

ABOVE: What was just an everyday scene on the Great Northern when photographed on August 2, 1955, has aged into a vintage look at a classic railroad (as well as a lineup of classic automobiles) that has been gone since 1970. We're high in the Cascade Mountains at Skykomish, Washington, as the eastbound *Cascadian* strolls into town during its all-day sashay from Seattle to Spokane, Washington. Compared to its fellow passenger trains on this route—the *Empire Builder* and the *Western Star*, both of which in at least one direction passed through the area in the cloak of darkness—the *Cascadian* was a relatively insignificant local run, but because of its daylight schedule the best from which to see nearly all the scenery GN's line had to offer in the 330 miles between Seattle and Spokane. Skykomish was also the western terminus for GN's electrified operations (note the overhead catenary lines in the above photo). On the 43-mile electrified stretch between Skykomish and Wenatchee, Washington, GN operated various types of electric locomotives, the largest of which were two 360-ton General Electric streamlined "motors" delivered to GN in 1947. One of them (RIGHT) stands at Skykomish between runs on July 31, 1955. Dieselization and a newly installed (in 1956) ventilation system in the Cascade Tunnel obviated the need for electrification, and the wires were de-energized exactly one year to the day after this photo was taken.—BOTH PHOTOS, MONTY POWELL.

93

ABOVE: The *Western Star* was the *Empire Builder*'s companion transcon, operating on a schedule that was more or less opposite that of the *Builder* (and for a time on a slightly different routing). For example, whereas the eastbound *Builder* made an early morning appearance in the Twin Cities before continuing to Chicago, the eastbound *Star* rolled into town in mid afternoon. Five Electro-Motive F-units have just brought the *Western Star* into Great Northern Station, hard against the Mississippi River in Minneapolis, on a summer afternoon in 1966. Most of the *Star* will terminate at St. Paul Union Depot, the next stop, but a couple of through cars will be handled to Chicago by Burlington's overnight *Black Hawk*.—JIM BOYD.

the *Builder* again. (The *Builder*'s earlier streamlined cars were reassigned to its companion train, the *Oriental Limited*, which was then renamed *Western Star*.)

In 1951, John Budd, son of GN's former president Ralph Budd, became the last president of the Great Northern. Under his reign, the dieselization program was completed, in 1957, ending all steam and electric operations. Budd continued to support the passenger train despite troubling signs of a nationwide decline in rail passenger revenues, ordering 22 new dome cars for *Empire Builder* service in 1955. The *Builder* in particular remained a class operation right to the end of the Great Northern in 1970, becoming widely acclaimed as the train of choice linking the Midwest with the Pacific Northwest. (Staunch aficionados of the *Builder*'s most-famous competitor, Northern Pacific's Chicago-Seattle/Portland *North Coast Limited*, would likely argue the claim.) Amtrak continues to operate the *Empire Builder* to this day, a testimony to the high reputation that this train established under the GN flag.

Budd also implemented new marketing strategies for freight traffic, and beginning early in the 1960s the railroad began ordering a new generation of diesel locomotives. The new locomotives, manufactured by General Electric and by Electro-Motive (GM) helped GN maintain its pre-eminence in freight transportation, as did the construction of a major new classification yard at Minot, North Dakota, and improved mainline relocations. In 1967, the railroad also underwent an image revamp, shedding its hallowed orange-and-green colors for the new "Big Sky Blue" and white livery.

By 1966, GN FOUNDER James J. Hill had been dead for a half century, but one of his longtime dreams—that of consolidating his GN, rival Northern Pacific, the GN-controlled CB&Q and the NP/GN-affiliated Spokane, Portland & Seattle into one giant railroad—was gaining momentum. This consolidation had first been attempted in 1904 and then again in 1927, but it failed. Not until 1970, following years of litigation, did the merger actually happen. On March 2 of that year, Burlington Northern was born and Great Northern and its fabled "Rocky" the mountain goat were consigned to the history books.

LEFT: Though often associated mainly with the northern tier of the U.S., the GN dipped down into America's heartland via a line that ran southwest out of St. Cloud, Minnesota, to Garrettson, South Dakota, where it split for Sioux Falls and Yankton, South Dakota, and Sioux City, Iowa. These routes served as gateways to connecting roads which headed southwest, at the same time providing additional access to America's bread belt. GN's engine facility at Sioux Falls is shown on a clean-air summer day in 1966.—RON LUNDSTROM. BELOW: Not only was GN a gateway between different regions of the U.S., it was also a link between the U.S. and Canada. The streamlined *International* was GN's ambassador train between Seattle and Vancouver, British Columbia. At Blaine, Washington, in June 1954, the northbound *International* skirts Boundary Bay just prior to leaving the country.—MONTY POWELL.

MAIN LINE OF MID-AMERICA

Illinois Central

The Illinois Central was (and is) a north-south railroad in an east-west world. Yet, that was a niche that called for transportation, and the "Main Line of Mid-America" filled it well. Although today's IC is a vital link between Chicago and the Gulf, the railroad's origins pre-date Chicago as a rail center. In the late 1840's, growing support for a great "Central Railroad" (which had been envisioned as early as 1836) was led in part by Senator Stephen A. Douglas. In 1850, President Millard Fillmore authorized land grants—the first to any U.S. railroad—for a line to be built between Dunleith (now East Dubuque) and Galena, both tucked in the rugged northwest corner of Illinois, and Cairo, on the Ohio River at the extreme southern tip of the state; a branch to Chicago was an afterthought. With its bustling lead mines, Galena was considered an important industrial center, and the Central Railroad would provide a year-round, ice-free link with Cairo, where transfer could be made to Gulf-bound boats.

When its charter was approved in 1851, the *Illinois Central Railroad* began construction of its "charter line" along the land grants. By the end of 1856, the railroad was completed between Dunleith and Cairo, 453 miles, as well as between Centralia and Chicago, 252 miles. At 705 miles, IC for several years enjoyed the spotlight as the world's longest railroad.

Unfortunately for Galena, its spotlight was fading. A financial panic in 1857 halted its industrial boom, forever rendering Galena's destiny to that of a quiet backwater burgh and—in the 20th Century—tourist center. Chicago, of course, wound up with a much-improved transportation artery to New Orleans, with IC connecting to its own steamship line at Cairo.

As IC went to war—the Civil War—one of the railroad's corporate lawyers, Abraham Lincoln, who served IC from 1853 to 1860, went on to become President of the United States. IC became a crucial artery for troops and supplies during the four-year conflict.

Following Galena's fall from industrial importance, the IC in search of other traffic sources extended itself beyond Dunleith into Iowa, reaching Sioux City in 1870 through lease of the Dubuque & Sioux City Railroad. The next logical step was to extend south from Cairo to New Orleans to create the first all-rail route (save for the ferrying of traffic across the Ohio River) between Chicago and a Gulf port. This was accomplished through a combination of purchases and leases of smaller railroads and new construction which brought IC's reach down through Jackson, Tennessee, and Jackson, Mississippi; a through route to New Orleans (ignoring a barge transfer across the Ohio River) was gained in 1873.

The IC map in this chapter reveals a thick web of routes in Mississippi. Most of these routes were developed or acquired in the late 1800s through a subsidiary railroad, the Yazoo & Mississippi Valley, which IC interests incorporated in 1882 to build west from Jackson (Mississippi) to Shreveport, Louisiana. In 1893 IC gained a Memphis-Louisville route by purchasing the Chesapeake & Ohio Southwestern. The Fulton (Kentucky)-Memphis segment of this line would become the preferred route for IC freight and passenger traffic moving north and south.

In 1886, IC incorporated the Chicago, Madison & Northern to fill a critical gap in the system: that between Chicago and the Charter Line at Freeport, Illinois. The gap was closed in 1891, and, along with a new branch to Wisconsin's state capital, IC now had its own direct line from Chicago west to central Iowa. Meanwhile, the 1889 completion of a rail bridge over the Ohio River at Cairo gave the IC true credence in its burgeoning role in north-south transportation. By 1895, the railroad was also serving St. Louis from the south; its Chicago-St. Louis line was completed in 1899.

ILLINOIS CENTRAL

PANAMA LIMITED ALL-PULLMAN STREAMLINER *Chicago • St. Louis • New Orleans*
CITY OF NEW ORLEANS ALL-COACH STREAMLINER *Chicago • St. Louis • New Orleans*
CITY OF MIAMI PULLMAN AND COACH STREAMLINER *Chicago • St. Louis • Florida*
GREEN DIAMOND PARLOR CAR AND COACH STREAMLINER *Chicago • Springfield • St. Louis*
LAND O'CORN ALL-COACH STREAMLINER *Chicago • Dubuque • Waterloo*

Main Line of Mid-America

IC entered the ballad books when it entered the 20th Century: On April 30, 1900, IC engineer John Luther "Casey" Jones was killed in a collision between his train, the southbound *New Orleans Special* (known locally as the "Cannonball"), and a southbound freight at Vaughan, Mississippi. Casey's efforts in slowing his train seconds before the crash saved many lives; his was the only one lost. The song "Casey Jones" was first chanted by a black IC engine-wiper, Wallace Saunders, who knew Casey, and eventually the song and Casey became an integral part of American folklore.

The 20th Century ushered in continued success and growth for IC. In 1906 the railroad reached Indianapolis, Indiana, and by 1908, Birmingham, Alabama. In 1928 IC constructed the Edgewood Cutoff as a bypass around Cairo, which had become a bottleneck. Much of IC's development in the late 19th and early 20th centuries could be attributed to Edward H. Harriman, who in 1883 was elected to the road's board of directors. Harriman, a well-known and highly regarded railroad magnate of the times, reigned over an empire that included Union Pacific, Southern Pacific, Chicago & Alton and Central of Georgia, all of which were enjoying the successes of the new century under Harriman influence.

The Illinois Central emerged as one of the most-respected railroads of the first half of the 20th Century, thanks in part to the leadership of one of its most-esteemed presidents, Charles Markham. During the 1920s, the railroad embarked on numerous improvements, including the electrification of its Chicago suburban train operations, the installation of heavier rail and stronger bridges throughout the system, the opening of a huge new freight-handling facility—Markham Yard—near Chicago, and the construction of an immense new shop complex at Paducah, Kentucky.

Symbolic of its high-speed steel boulevard linking North and South was the crack *Panama Limited*, inaugurated in 1911 between Chicago and New Orleans. The *Panama* wasn't IC's only passenger run, of course. In addition to a bevy of other trains along the Chicago-Memphis-New Orleans route, IC offered extensive passenger services between Chicago and Iowa, St. Louis, and Florida.

With its connections to the Gulf at one end and a sprawl of lines into Midwest farm markets at the other, small wonder that IC carried a tremendous amount of fruit and produce. Interestingly, the banana was key to IC perishable-freight revenues. Here was a highly sensitive fruit that, until the building of the IC, could only be enjoyed by Gulf residents. Once the IC opened for business, bananas quickly came into high demand all up and down the system. Banana traffic blossomed for the next several decades. During 1947, IC moved a record 52,757 cars of bananas making it the leading banana carrier in all the world. Naturally, speed was of essence in banana transport, and IC moved the green fruit in solid strings of refrigerator cars—high-speed trains that demanded priority even over passenger liners.

IC barely survived the Depression, but it entered the World War II era as a financially stable, if conservative, carrier. For this and other reasons—not the least of which was that IC served several coal fields—IC was not as quick to dieselize freight operations as were other carriers. Nevertheless, IC was among the earliest to experiment with the infant power source, purchasing its first diesels in 1929 and rostering some 20 diesels (all switchers) by 1936. IC was also a streamliner pioneer, purchasing its homely diesel-powered

Most of the steam locomotives rostered by Illinois Central had relatively clean lines, a trait particularly noticeable in the road's far-flung fleet of Mountain types (4-8-2's) such as the 2524 storming out of East St. Louis in 1949. These fast high-drivered Mountains were used in both manifest freight and high-speed passenger service. Steam on the IC lasted late by U.S. standards—some IC steam operated down in the Kentucky coal fields as late as 1960. Nonetheless, other parts of the railroad had been dieselized by the mid-to-late 1950s.—GERALD CARLSON, COLLECTION OF MIKE SCHAFER.

ILLINOIS CENTRAL AT A GLANCE

Headquarters: Chicago

Mileage:
1950: 4,779
1995: 2,732 (including trackage-rights routes)

Locomotive fleet as of 1963: 629 diesels

Rolling stock as of 1963:
Freight cars: 49,226 **Passenger cars:** 857

Principal lines circa 1950:
Chicago-New Orleans via Mattoon and Carbondale, Ill., and Grenada, Miss.
Memphis-New Orleans via Vicksburg, Miss, and Baton Rouge, La.
Memphis-Jackson, Miss., via Greenwood, Miss.
Fulton, Ky.-Birmingham, Ala.
Freeport-Centralia, Ill., via Clinton and Vandalia
Chicago-Omaha, Neb.
Tara (Fort Dodge)-Sioux City, Iowa
Cherokee, Iowa-Sioux Falls, S. Dak.
Manchester-Cedar Rapids, Iowa
Waterloo, Iowa-Albert Lea, Minn.
Centralia, Ill.-Madison, Wis.
Gilman, Ill.-St. Louis
St. Louis-Du Quoin, Ill.
Edgewood, Ill.-Fulton, Ky.
Fulton-Louisville, Ky., via Paducah
Effingham, Ill.-Indianapolis, Ind.
Mattoon-Peoria, Ill. via Decatur
Jackson-Gulfport, Miss.
Meridian, Miss.-Shreveport, La.

Notable passenger trains:
Chickasaw (Memphis-St. Louis/Chicago)
City of Miami (Chicago/St. Louis-Miami/St. Petersburg, Fla.; joint with Central of Georgia, Atlantic Coast Line and Florida East Coast)
City of New Orleans (Chicago/St. Louis/Louisville-New Orleans)
Daylight (Chicago-St. Louis)
Delta Express (Memphis-Vicksburg, Miss.)
Green Diamond (Chicago-St. Louis)
Hawkeye (Chicago-Sioux City)
Iowan (Chicago-Sioux City)
Irvin S. Cobb (Louisville-New Orleans)
Kentucky Cardinal (Louisville-Memphis)
Land O' Corn (Chicago-Waterloo, Iowa)
Louisiane (Chicago/St. Louis-New Orleans)
Magnolia Star (Chicago-New Orleans)
Mid-American (Chicago-Memphis)
Night Diamond (Chicago-St. Louis)
Panama Limited (Chicago/St. Louis-New Orleans)
Planter (Louisville-Memphis)
Seminole (Chicago-Jacksonville, Fla., via Birmingham and Columbus, Ga.)
Southwestern Limited/Northeastern Limited (Meridian-Shreveport)

Illinois Central's highly esteemed chocolate-and-orange passenger paint scheme was introduced in 1941 with the delivery of new Electro-Motive diesels for the *Panama Limited*, which was re-equipped as a streamliner the following year. Save for the replacement of IC's long-traditional diamond emblem, the scheme remained virtually unchanged to the end of IC intercity passenger service in 1971. In this 1967 scene, GM Electro-Motive E9 4042—still sporting the green diamond herald—pauses at Rockford, Illinois, with the overnight Chicago-Sioux City *Hawkeye*.—MIKE SCHAFER.

ILLINOIS CENTRAL RAILROAD

ILLINOIS CENTRAL
Main Line of Mid-America

Indicates Double Track
Scale of Miles
0   25   50   75   100
Geographically correct map
Copyright by Rand McNally & Company

Green Diamond streamliner in 1936.

These exceptions aside, steam was the choice of power for most mainline IC freight well into the 1950s, thanks largely to the skills and efforts of shop forces at Paducah, which maintained and repaired hundreds of IC locomotives. Most of all, Paducah Shops were known for rebuilding IC's steam fleet into a new generation of powerful locomotives, transforming World War I-era 2-10-2's into high-speed 4-8-2's.

Mainline diesel application on the IC began on passenger trains. Following the *Green Diamond*, IC's first true road diesel was an Electro-Motive E6A built in 1940 for the new streamliner *City of Miami*, which operated between Chicago and Miami jointly with Central of Georgia, Atlantic Coast Line and Florida East Coast. More EMC passenger diesels arrived the following year for the *Panama Limited*. That was the extent of dieselization until after World War II, when additional passenger diesels came on the property. IC did not receive its first road freight diesels until 1951, and not until 1960 was the railroad fully dieselized with an armada of black "Geeps" (Electro-Motive Division GP7, GP9 and GP18 locomotives).

One new innovation the IC did embrace fairly quickly was the streamlining of its pas-

ABOVE: At the lower end of IC's spectrum of passenger service were the dozens of daily suburban trains that fed downtown Chicago. IC's commuter service was quite extensive, and it was one of the few electrified suburban services in the U.S. outside the East Coast—and the only one in Chicago. Three lines funneled trains into IC's Randolph Street Station at the foot of the Prudential Building in the heart of downtown Chicago. On June 14, 1966, an outbound two-car electric commuter train is pulling away from Van Buren Station, just south of the Art Institute. In the early days of the IC, this area was still part of Lake Michigan.—WILLIAM D. MIDDLETON.
RIGHT: The southbound *Green Diamond* coasts into Kankakee, Illinois, in July 1959. The *Green Diamond* was IC's first streamliner, introduced in 1936 between Chicago and St. Louis. In 1947 it received new equipment, and in 1968 the run was cut back to Springfield, Illinois, and renamed the *Governor's Special*.—R. P. Meyer.

senger fleet. Aside from the 1936 introduction of the *Green Diamond* and the 1940 debut of the *City of Miami*, the *Panama Limited* received new streamlined equipment (the first to wear the railroad's dazzling new brown-and-orange livery) in 1942. Shortly after World War II ended, IC embarked on a massive program of streamlining, ordering dozens of new lightweight cars from Pullman-Standard and at the same time frugally rebuilding many older heavyweight cars into pseudo-streamlined cars at its Burnside car shops in Chicago.

Among the new streamliners launched in the halcyon postwar years was the storied *City of New Orleans*—the "Great Dayliner", so nicknamed because its fast daylight run. The *City* departed IC's lakefront Central Station in Chicago at 8 a.m. and arrived New Orleans shortly before midnight the same day—16 hours to cover 921 miles including some two dozen scheduled passenger stops, a feat made possible in part by IC's well-maintained dou-

ABOVE: IC dieselized its freight operations almost entirely with a vast fleet of GP7 and GP9 locomotives from builder Electro-Motive. Showing IC's conservative side, these "Geeps" wore a utilitarian black scheme with white stripes and the green diamond emblem. Two of the 1750-hp. units wheel a hopper train south through Chebanse, Illinois, on IC's high-speed Chicago-Champaign-Carbondale main line in June 1957. IC also used the versatile Geeps in passenger service, equipping several of them with steam generators necessary for passenger-train heating. Their limited speeds (65/83 mph versus 117 mph for IC's regular passenger diesels) relegated the Geeps to secondary passenger services, however.—MONTY POWELL.

RIGHT: In 1966 Illinois Central unveiled a new image. In a complete reversal from austere black, freight locomotives began wearing an orange-and-white livery that included the road's new "split-rail" I/C emblem. Two Electro-Motive GP38AC diesels clad in the new colors drop downhill into Dixon, Illinois, with Freeport-Clinton train No. 373 in 1972.—MIKE MCBRIDE. BELOW: Following a lackluster 15-year merger with Gulf, Mobile & Ohio as the Illinois Central Gulf Railroad, the Illinois Central re-emerged in 1987, complete with the old black-and-white scheme (updated with a still-newer herald). Two new GM SD70 diesels lead symbol freight GLNO (for Glenn Yard/Chicago-New Orleans) south out of Chicago in December 1995.—GORDON SMITH.

ble-track speedway whose official speed limit was as high as 100 mph in parts of Illinois.

IC continued to prosper after World War II under the leadership of Wayne A. Johnston. The railroad remained staunchly conservative throughout Johnston's 21-year (1945-1966) tenure, but that trait proved an asset. Johnston always ran a tight ship. From his office high up in Central Station, Chicago, he could see the tail end of the *Panama Limited* as it sat in the depot for boarding prior to its long-traditional daily 5 p.m. departure. If the train was still visible after 5 p.m., Johnston was immediately on the phone to depot personnel to see what the delay was all about.

New management after 1966 pointed IC in a new direction—and with a completely new image. Out went IC's long-famous diamond emblem and somber black paint worn by freight diesels, and in came a bright new orange-and-white freight scheme and clever split-rail logo. New locomotives were purchased, freight operations rearranged and passenger services rationalized.

In 1971, IC became a member of the new National Railroad Passenger Corporation—Amtrak—turning the core of its passenger services over to that carrier and discontinuing the rest. In August 1972, IC merged with Gulf, Mobile & Ohio forming the Illinois Central Gulf Railroad. The IC was now history—or so it was thought. Despite the economies of merger, the union was not particularly successful, and ICG sunk into unprofitability to the point where parent IC Industries announced its intent to sell the railroad.

Potential buyers balked at the prospect of acquiring a network of marginal lines, so in the 1980s, new management took ICG in a new direction by selling off large chunks of the railroad. Five major sales and a number of minor ones spawned new regional railroads like Chicago, Missouri & Western and Paducah & Louisville as ICG shrank to a 2,800-mile Chicago-New Orleans "core" system. One of the largest transactions was the 1985 transfer of the entire Chicago-Iowa network to new regional operator, Chicago Central & Pacific.

But history does occasionally repeat itself as a new railroad emerged from this reorganization: the Illinois Central! The "Gulf" was dropped from the name, and black diesels returned on the new IC, which embarked on

an aggressive program to streamline operations and labor relations. As a result, the IC of the 1990s became a leader in the railroad industry, boasting one of the lowest operating ratios of any U.S. railroad. Then in 1996, in a bizarre twist of irony, IC announced its intention to buy back the Chicago-Iowa lines.

Considering the fact that the *City of New Orleans* still cruises IC rails between Chicago and New Orleans, albeit under the Amtrak banner, and that black diesels still speed freight between Chicago and the Gulf and Iowa, the IC story has nearly come full circle.

ABOVE: Continuing a service that was soon to be a quarter century old, the *City of New Orleans* accelerates away from Chicago's Central Station (whose giant diamond neon sign is just visible against the Standard Oil sign in the background) on a summer morning in 1971. Although now being operated under Amtrak auspices, IC still provided the equipment, so the *City* looked much as it did when inaugurated in 1947. Top speeds of 100 mph through Illinois will put the *City* into New Orleans shortly after midnight.—MIKE SCHAFER.

Louisville & Nashville

Like the name says, it all started in Louisville, Kentucky. The growing Ohio River port was anxious to sponsor a railroad, so in 1850 the Commonwealth of Kentucky granted a charter for the Louisville & Nashville Railroad to build between those two points as well as to Lebanon, Kentucky, and Memphis, Tennessee, a growing port on the Mississippi. The first segment of railroad—that between Louisville and Lebanon—opened later the same year, but owing to various problems it took until 1859 to open the entire route between Louisville and Nashville. Operations to Memphis began in 1861.

The Civil War in effect divided the L&N. With Kentucky as a Union state and Tennessee in the Confederacy, much of the railroad was destroyed during the early years of the conflict. L&N rebuilt, and after the war set its sights on expansion to ward off competing railroads. By 1872, L&N had extended itself south to Montgomery, Alabama, through acquisition of a string of little railroads south of Nashville that had been building since about the start of the Civil War.

Expansion accelerated as the war years receded. In 1879 L&N purchased the Evansville, Henderson & St. Louis, which didn't actually go to St. Louis but it got the L&N north to the gateway city of Evansville, Ind. At about the same time, L&N pushed into New Orleans with the purchase of the Montgomery & Mobile between those two points, and the New Orleans, Mobile & Texas.

In about 1880, L&N gained control of the Nashville, Chattanooga & St. Louis, which was attempting to establish a through route between Atlanta and St. Louis. Up to this point, NC&StL had been considered a rival of the L&N; from that time forward, it was an ally and eventually an integral part of the L&N. Early on, L&N took NC&StL's Evansville-St. Louis line, adding it to its own expanding network. Now L&N reached one of the most important rail centers in the U.S., St. Louis.

The eastern side of the L&N was expanding as well. In 1881, L&N bought the Louisville, Cincinnati & Lexington Railroad, giving it a through route from Louisville to Cincinnati (known as the "Short Line") and a branch to Lexington through the state capital of Frankfort. Meanwhile the Lebanon branch was extended east to Livingston and south through Corbin and into Tennessee, reaching Jellico in 1883 where connection was made with the Southern Railway.

Like the main line south from Louisville to New Orleans, L&N's main line south from Cincinnati to Atlanta was pieced together through purchases and construction. In 1891 L&N bought the 20-year-old Kentucky Central Railroad, whose spine ran north and south between Covington, Kentucky (across the Ohio from Cincinnati), and a connection with L&N's now-extended Lebanon branch near Livingston. (The KC purchase also included a line from Lexington to Paris, Kentucky, the latter also on the Ohio River.)

The L&N now had a direct through route from Cincinnati to the Tennessee border. Shortly following the turn of the century, the L&N began building south from the border to Knoxville, there eventually linking up with two railroads—the Knoxville Southern and the Marietta & North Georgia—that the L&N would purchase in 1902 to bring it to Marietta, Georgia, 21 miles out of Atlanta. From Marietta, L&N used Western & Atlantic tracks to reach Atlanta. The Cincinnati-Atlanta line opened as a through route in 1905.

The Corbin-Atlanta line was rugged, particularly south of Etowah, Tennessee, where the line became known as the "Hook & Eye" account of its sharp curves and Hiwassee Loop, where the track looped over itself to gain elevation in a confined area. L&N bypassed the Hook & Eye by constructing a better-engineered route in 1906 between Etowah and Cartersville.

WINTER — 1955-56

L&N

PASSENGER TRAIN TIME TABLES

LOUISVILLE AND NASHVILLE RAILROAD

DECEMBER 16, 1955

FACING PAGE: It's the post-midnight hour at Mobile, Alabama, in the late 1960s as L&N's *Pan-American*, just in from New Orleans, gets a nose job before resuming its northward journey. By the breakfast hour, the *"Pan"* will be at Birmingham, Alabama; during the noon hour, it will call at Nashville, Tennessee, and by the dinner hour, at Louisville, Kentucky. By 10 p.m., the *Pan* will reach its final destination, Cincinnati, Ohio.—JIM BOYD. FACING PAGE INSET: L&N passenger diesels await to take their respective trains out of Louisville in the summer of 1965.—RON LUNDSTROM. LEFT: L&N's timetable covers changed little during the postwar years. This one is from 1955.

L&N's growth in the late 19th and early 20th centuries included the development of numerous branch lines in every state served by Old Reliable, but two—both of them running east off the Cincinnati-Atlanta main line—are of particular note. In 1910 the Lexington & Eastern Railroad came under the wing of L&N as a subsidiary; it ran east from Lexington, crossing L&N's Atlanta-Cincinnati main at Winchester and augering through Irvine into the eastern Kentucky coal fields around Jackson. L&N extended its L&E nearly to the Virginia border in 1912; this line and its various coal branches were collectively known as the "EK", for eastern Kentucky.

The second branch of note—actually comprised of a web of branches—was that which became L&N's Cumberland Valley Division. L&N began constructing the Cumberland Valley line out of Corbin in 1886 with twofold intentions: (1) to tap the rich coal and iron-ore reserves of eastern Kentucky and western Virginia and (2) to reach the Norfolk & Western building west out of Bluefield, Virginia. The line dipped into Tennessee to cross Big Stone Gap and then turned north into Virginia to reach the N&W, which it did in 1891.

The EK and the Cumberland Valley line provided an enormous amount of coal traffic for generating stations all over the Eastern U.S. Although considered "branches," the EK line had (and still have) the appearance of main lines, with heavy rail and in some places double track over which numerous heavy trains pass.

The opening of the Cincinnati-Atlanta line in 1905 pretty much completed L&N's trunk-route network—for most of the first half of the 20th Century anyway. Like most other major railroads of the first two decades of the 20th Century, L&N turned its focus on upgrading physical plant with heavier track and new signal systems and acquiring new locomotives and rolling stock. In 1917, for example, L&N opened DeCoursey Yard near Latonia, Kentucky. Located some seven miles south of Cincinnati, DeCoursey served as L&N's major yard and engine-servicing facility for that metropolitan area, superceding a rag-tag collection of older, smaller yards scattered about the Queen City area.

South Louisville—a long-established older yard and engine facility near L&N's birthplace city—was another heartbeat for L&N operations. Whereas most railroads of the period relied on major outside manufacturers—firms like American Locomotive Company (Alco, Schenectady, New York) and American Car & Foundry (St. Louis)—to construct the bulk of their locomotives and cars, L&N called on its own work force for much of the equipment built early in the 20th Century. For example, South Louisville Shops had constructed in excess of 400 steam locomotives by 1923.

STRADDLING THE North and South, L&N was often the middleman—and the endman, too—in much of the nation's Midwest-Southeast freight and

BELOW: L&N's signature steam locomotive were the M-1-class 2-8-4's (Berkshires)—the "Big Emmas." Strutting through Paris, Kentucky, Big Emma No. 1962 has southbound freight in tow. The date is August 17, 1951.—R. D. ACTON SR.

ABOVE: Scrubbers are at it again, this time cleaning the *Georgian* during its layover at Atlanta Union Station in April 1963. A heavyweight reclining-seat coach (second car back) mingles with an otherwise streamlined set of cars. In the early evening, the *Georgian* will depart for Chicago.—ROGER PUTA, COLLECTION OF MEL FINZER.

LOUISVILLE & NASHVILLE AT A GLANCE

Headquarters: Louisville, Kentucky

Mileage
1950: 4,779

Locomotives owned as of 1963:
Diesel: 732

Rolling stock owned as of 1963:
Freight cars: 59,077   Passenger: 483

Principal lines circa 1950:
Cincinnati-New Orleans via Louisville, Nashville, Lewisburg, Tenn., and Birmingham
Nashville-St. Louis via Evansville, Ind.
Louisville-Evansville
Memphis Junction, Ky. (Bowling Green)-Memphis
Cincinnati-Atlanta via Knoxville, Tenn., and Cartersville, Ga.
Flomaton, Ala.-Chattahoochie, Fla.
Anchorage-Hazard, Ky., via Lexington
Corbin-Baxter, Ky.
Lebanon Junction-Sinks, Ky.

Notable passenger trains (alphabetically):
Azalean (New York-New Orleans via Montgomery; joint with Pennsylvania, Southern Railway, and Atlanta & West Point)
Crescent (New York-New Orleans via Montgomery; joint with Pennsylvania, Southern Railway, and Atlanta & West Point)
Dixie Flagler (Chicago-Miami via Evansville, Nashville and Atlanta)
Dixie Flyer (Chicago-Florida via Evansville, Nashville and Atlanta)
Dixieland (Chicago-Miami via Louisville, Nashville and Montgomery)
Flamingo (Cincinnati-Jacksonville via Corbin, Ky.)
Georgian (Chicago/St. Louis-Atlanta)
Gulf Wind (New Orleans-Jacksonville; joint with Atlantic Coast Line)
Humming Bird (Chicago/St. Louis/Cincinnati-New Orleans and Memphis; joint with Chicago & Eastern Illinois)
Pan-American (Cincinnati-Memphis/New Orleans)
Piedmont Limited (New York-New Orleans via Montgomery; joint with Pennsylvania, Southern Railway, and Atlanta & West Point)
Southland (Detroit-Florida via Louisville and Corbin)
South Wind (Chicago-Miami via Louisville, Nashville and Montgomery)

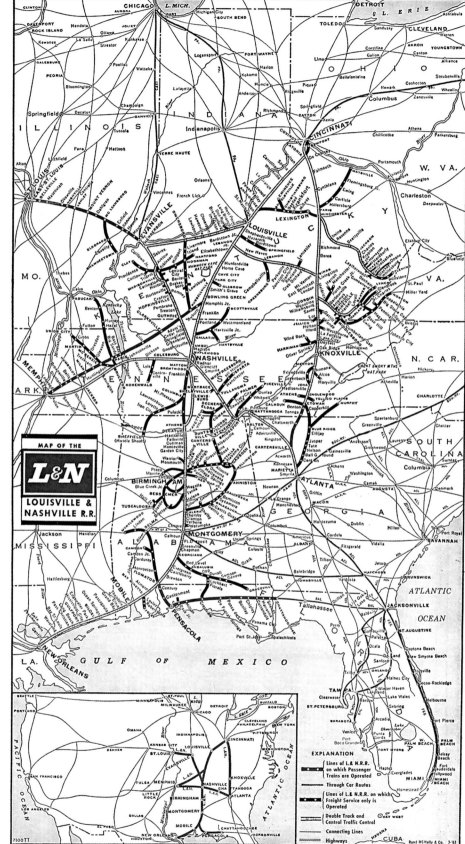

MAP OF THE
L&N
LOUISVILLE &
NASHVILLE R.R.

EXPLANATION
Lines of L. & N.R.R. on which Passenger Trains are Operated
Through Car Routes
Lines of L.& N.R.R. on which Freight Service only is Operated
Double Track and Central Traffic Control
Connecting Lines
Highways

Rand McNally & Co.   3-'63

passenger transport. Traffic off the Pennsylvania and Baltimore & Ohio at Cincinnati and Louisville, the Chicago & Eastern Illinois at Evansville, and off several Western carriers at St. Louis was funneled over the L&N to Gulf or river ports or to Atlanta where Central of Georgia, Atlantic Coast Line and Southern forwarded it to the Eastern seaboard and Florida.

L&N operated a widely varied fleet of passenger trains, the most-prestigious of which was the *Pan-American*, a coach-and-sleeper run introduced in 1921 between Cincinnati and New Orleans. Named in recognition of L&N's' role in forwarding traffic to and from Central and South America through Gulf ports, the "*Pan*", as it was known locally, was highly touted as an "all-steel train" during an era when wood passenger cars were still abundant.

Although many an L&N passenger train had the duty of linking on-line cities, Louisville & Nashville was first and foremost an interline carrier, working closely with several other railroads in providing through passenger service between the North and South. Trains like the New York New Orleans *Crescent* and *Piedmont Limited* involved the cooperation of four roads: Pennsylvania, Southern Railway, Atlanta & West Point and L&N, which handled those trains between Montgomery and New Orleans.

Nowhere was L&N's interline role more evident than in the highly competitive Midwest-Florida market, and to a lesser degree the Midwest-Gulf corridor. Several Midwest and Northeast carriers boasted Florida trains and runs to New Orleans, and L&N was usually a key player, although in some cases it only provided a relatively short segment of route. The famed *Dixie Flyer* was once a flagship between Chicago, St. Louis and Florida, operated by Chicago & Eastern Illinois, L&N, NC&StL,

ABOVE: A trio of six-axle General Electric locomotives leading a coal train near Harlan, Kentucky, in the spring of 1974 "hole up" in a passing siding to await an opposing train. This was L&N's line over the Appalachians to the Norfolk & Western connection at Norton, Virginia. Coal was long a major commodity for L&N, with tremendous quantities of "black diamonds" mined in eastern Kentucky coal fields where L&N had much prominence.—JIM BOYD.
RIGHT: The *Pan American* awaits its southbound departure from Louisville Union Station during the summer of 1965. L&N shared the elegant stub-end depot—which still stands, restored—with the Pennsylvania Railroad, Chesapeake & Ohio, and Monon. The L&N headquarters building was right next door to the east.—RON LUNDSTROM.

Central of Georgia, ACL and Florida East Coast. A better-known train in later years was the *South Wind*, a new Chicago-Miami streamliner introduced in 1940 running over the Pennsy to Louisville, then L&N, NC&StL, ACL and FEC to Miami. L&N was a latecomer to the streamliner bandwagon, waiting until after World War II to introduce its first own streamlined trains: the *Humming Bird* and the *Georgian*. When inaugurated in 1946, the *Bird* was a Cincinnati-New Orleans run and the *Georgian* an Atlanta-St. Louis train operated jointly with NC&StL. By the early 1950s, both trains boasted Chicago sections, operating over the C&EI. The 1950 streamlining of the *Crescent Limited* was much more a joint project between its operators, with L&N owning only a few of the fleet of streamlined cars used in the service.

COAL WAS ALWAYS a prime commodity hauled by L&N, but that did not prevent the railroad from realizing the extraordinary importance of dieselization. L&N's first diesels arrived before World War II, and although the railroad purchased some modern steam power as late as 1949, L&N was all diesel by 1957.

Although L&N may not have been consid-

ered one of the more progressive railroads in postwar America, it was one of the earliest in that period to enter an expansion-through-merger development phase. August 30, 1957, signaled the start of a "new" L&N era when Old Reliable merged with "The Dixie Line" (adopting that road's slogan in the process) the NC&StL. Considering the long-time affiliation between the two roads, the amalgamation was hardly a surprise. Now L&N had a direct route between Nashville, Chattanooga and Atlanta and between Nashville and the Memphis gateway, although coordinated opera-

TOP: Morning at Cincinnati in the late 1950s finds L&N train No. 33, the *Southland*, departing Union Terminal behind a pair of passenger diesels wearing their as-delivered original L&N scheme of dark blue and cream. Although essentially just a Cincinnati-Atlanta train for the L&N, the *Southland* offered connecting through cars from Chicago and Detroit and beyond Atlanta to Florida points.—AL SCHULTZ.
ABOVE: Less glamorous was this two-car local behind L&N Pacific No. 231 at Knoxville, Tennessee, in 1949.—RAILROAD AVENUE ENTERPRISES.

ABOVE: The eastern Kentucky coal fields have served L&N and its successors well. On a sunny afternoon in April 1979, a westbound coal train sweeps around a curve east of Ravenna, Kentucky, having just passed a eastbound train (in the distance). L&N locomotives are already shedding their traditional L&N Confederate gray and yellow colors for that of the affiliated Family Lines.—MIKE SCHAFER. RIGHT: A EMD GP30 diesel stands at DeCoursey Yard near Cincinnati in 1965. DeCoursey was a principal yard for L&N, but it lost its importance after CSX Transportation—L&N's successor—opened its huge new Queensgate Yard in Cincinnati in the 1980s.—RON LUNDSTROM.

tions between the two roads and those points had existed for decades.

Then in 1969 L&N got a coveted entry to Chicago by purchasing affiliate C&EI's main line between Evansville and Chicago. At about the same time, L&N acquired 140 miles of trackage of erstwhile shortline Tennessee Central. Not content with just one entrance to Chicago, L&N merged the Monon (MOE-non) Railroad into its system in 1971, giving L&N a direct shot to Chicago from Louisville.

L&N had a long-time affiliation with the Atlantic Coast Line, which in 1967 merged with Seaboard Air Line to become Seaboard Coast Line. The holdings of SCL Industries, parent of the SCL Railroad, included L&N, the Clinchfield Railroad and the "Georgia Group" (Western Railway of Alabama, Georgia Railroad, Atlanta & West Point), and together in the 1970s they became the Family Lines. In 1980, Family Lines became affiliated with the Chessie System (Chesapeake & Ohio, B&O and Western Maryland), and together these railroads became a part of CSX Corporation. The end came for L&N in 1982 when it and SCL were formally merged, forming the short-lived Seaboard System —itself merged into CSX only five years later.

BELOW: With less than six months left to live, an anemic *Pan-American* flies high above an Ohio River tributary near Walton, Kentucky. Two EMD passenger diesels are more than sufficient for hustling the single baggage car, coach, and diner toward Louisville. The train will expand slightly at Louisville where a sleeper for New Orleans will be shunted on behind the diner. On April 30/May 1, 1971, the north- and southbound *Pans* would make their final trips as the new Amtrak assumed most U.S. intercity passenger-train operations.—ROBERT P. SCHMIDT.

New York Central

New York Central was one of the five "super railroads" that dominated U.S. railroading during the first 60 years of the 20th Century (others: Santa Fe, Union Pacific, Pennsylvania, and Southern Pacific).

If you superimpose a map of the New York Central System over that of the Pennsylvania Railroad, you'll see why these two giants were at one time arch rivals. Just about everywhere the Pennsy went, at least west of Buffalo, so did Central. But NYC was in many ways a mirror image of PRR. Pennsy painted its *Broadway Limited*, inside and out, in warm, friendly colors; Central cloaked its haute *20th Century Limited* in a swank combination of grays, whites and blacks. Pennsy designed and built a much of its own equipment; NYC preferred to rely on the tried-and-true expertise of independent locomotive and car manufacturers. Pennsy charged up, over and through the Alleghenies; NYC followed an almost-gradeless "water-level route" between the East Coast and the Midwest.

The "system" in NYC's title holds key to the railroad's impressive (for the Northeast and Midwest, anyway) width and breadth: It was comprised of several rather large subsidiary companies whose day-to-day operations were closely coordinated so as to provide seamless service throughout—a true system. Nucleus of that system was the New York Central Railroad, which had its very humble beginnings as the Mohawk & Hudson Railroad, opened in 1831 to connect Albany with Schenectady, a mere 17 miles distant.

Shortly after, an all-rail route connecting Albany with Buffalo was proposed—to the chagrin of New York State, which had spent heavily to build and open (in 1826) the Erie Canal between the two commercial centers. As if to sneak an all-rail route into the picture, several short railroads were separately incorporated and constructed to link various town

New York Central
The Scenic Water Level Route

Effective December 7, 1947
Form 1001

NEW YORK CENTRAL SYSTEM

pairs that lay between the west end of the M&H and Buffalo. Their names said it all: the Syracuse & Utica, the Auburn & Rochester, and so forth. By 1841, seven end-to-end railroads were providing coordinated through service between Albany and Buffalo. The ultimate indignation was that they were required to pay tolls to the Erie Canal. In 1853 this string of railroads plus a few others were merged to form the New York Central Railroad.

Enter Cornelius Vanderbilt, one of the most famous (some would say infamous) of 19th Century rail barons. Vanderbilt gained control of the NYC and in 1853 merged it with his Hudson River Railroad, which had opened between New York City and Albany in 1851. The result was the New York Central & Hudson River Railroad; eventually this was merged with another Vanderbilt interest, the New York & Harlem. By the end of the 1800s, NYC&HR had built and acquired lines which took it into the northern part of its home state and into Montreal.

Another company that figured closely in the development of the NYC was the New York, West Shore & Buffalo, a Pennsylvania Railroad concern which had built a line closely parallel to the NYC&HR all the way from New York to Buffalo. The West Shore was regarded by Vanderbilt as a surreptitious attempt by the mighty PRR to invade his territory, which it probably was.

In retaliation, Vanderbilt interests began building a line parallel to PRR's main line through the Alleghenies, but construction stopped when NYC gained control of the West Shore in the late 1800s. The aborted line through the Alleghenies later served as right-of-way for part of the Pennsylvania Turnpike.

To reach Chicago, the NYC&HR acquired control of the Lake Shore & Michigan Southern, itself a compilation of several smaller roads (some already under NYC&HR influence) that formed a route between Buffalo and Chicago via Toledo, Ohio, and South Bend,

FACING PAGE: Two streamliners of New York Central's once-far-flung "Great Steel Fleet"—as its passenger train network was called during the postwar streamliner era—sweep into Chicago's suburban Englewood station during the summer of 1967. At left is the eastbound *Twilight Limited*, less than half an hour into its afternoon Chicago-Detroit run; at right, an hour-late *Chicagoan* from New York City is on the final approach to La Salle Street station at Chicago's Loop.—MIKE SCHAFER. FACING PAGE INSET: Central's familiar oval emblem graced many a Midwest and Eastern depot; this was on the facade of Dayton (Ohio) Union Station.—ROGER PUTA, COLLECTION OF MEL FINZER. LEFT: This NYC timetable from 1947 featured the road's famed *20th Century Limited*s passing under a moon-beamed sky.

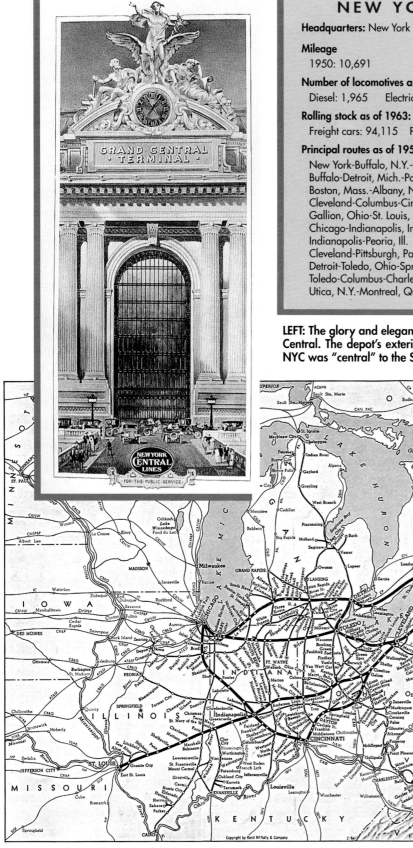

NEW YORK CENTRAL SYSTEM AT A GLANCE

Headquarters: New York City

Mileage
1950: 10,691

Number of locomotives as of 1963:
Diesel: 1,965   Electric: 65

Rolling stock as of 1963:
Freight cars: 94,115   Passenger cars: 2,905

Principal routes as of 1950:
New York-Buffalo, N.Y.-Cleveland, Ohio-Chicago
Buffalo-Detroit, Mich.-Porter, Ind. (Chicago)
Boston, Mass.-Albany, N.Y.
Cleveland-Columbus-Cincinnati, Ohio
Gallion, Ohio-St. Louis, Mo.
Chicago-Indianapolis, Ind.-Cincinnati
Indianapolis-Peoria, Ill.
Cleveland-Pittsburgh, Pa.
Detroit-Toledo, Ohio-Springfield, Ohio
Toledo-Columbus-Charleston, W.Va.
Utica, N.Y.-Montreal, Que.

Notable passenger trains (alphabetically):
Chicagoan (New York-Cleveland-Chicago)
Chicago Mercury (Chicago-Detroit)
Cincinnati Mercury (Cleveland-Cincinnati
Cleveland Mercury (Detroit-Cleveland)
Cleveland Limited (New York-Cleveland
Commodore Vanderbilt (New York-Chicago)
Detroiter (New York-Detroit)
Detroit Mercury (Cleveland-Detroit)
Empire State Express (New York-Buffalo)
James Whitcomb Riley (Chicago-Cincinnati)
Knickerbocker (New York-St. Louis)
Lake Shore Limited (New York-Cleveland-Chicago)
The *Michigan* (Chicago-Detroit)
Motor City Special (Chicago-Detroit)
New England States (Chicago-Cleveland-Boston)
Ohio State Limited (New York-Cleveland-Cincinnati)
Pacemaker (New York-Cleveland-Chicago)
Southwestern Limited (New York-St. Louis)
20th Century Limited (New York-Chicago)
Twilight Limited (Chicago-Detroit)
Wolverine (Chicago-Detroit-New York)

LEFT: The glory and elegance of Grand Central Terminal is apparent in this 1920s art plate issued by New York Central. The depot's exterior has changed little since its construction, save for decades of city grime. **BELOW:** NYC was "central" to the State of New York, but it was also a prominent carrier in Ohio and Indiana.

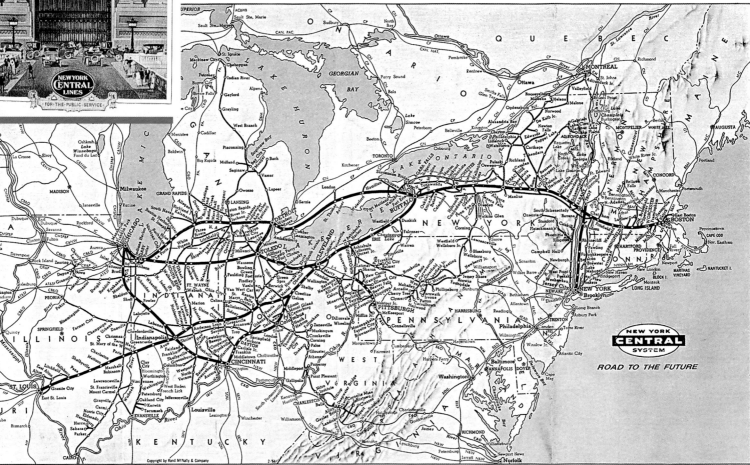

Indiana. Formal merger between NYC&HR and LS&MS didn't occur until 1914, and the resulting "new" name was—New York Central Railroad.

The important port city of Boston was a logical target for NYC&HR, and the easy way to get there was to buy one of two railroads already connecting the Albany region with Boston: the Fitchburg Railroad or the Boston & Albany. At the turn of the century, NYC&HR leased the latter (the Fitchburg later became part of Boston & Maine). Sensitive to local interests, the New York Central let B&A retain much of its own identity—but maintained closely coordinated services—right up until after World War II. Not until 1961 was the B&A formally merged into NYC.

NYC's primary stake in Michigan was through the Michigan Central, whose principal route was between Detroit and Chicago via Kalamazoo. NYC didn't lease the MC until 1930, but it certainly had influence on the MC for years prior: Vanderbilt had owned stock in MC since 1869. Further, one of MC's leased railroads was the Canada Southern, owned by Vanderbilt himself. The CS connected Windsor, Ontario (across the Detroit River from Detroit), with Niagara Falls, Ontario, and Buffalo. Together with MC, the CS gave Central an alternate route between Buffalo and Chicago.

Central's presence in Ohio, Indiana and Illinois was strengthened through two major purchases: the Toledo & Ohio Central and the Cleveland, Cincinnati, Chicago & St. Louis—better known (and easier said) as the "Big Four Route." NYC&HR's lease of the T&OC circa 1910 gave Central a route from Toledo to Columbus and into West Virginia coal fields. The Big Four was—surprise!—another Vanderbilt interest.

Though NYC didn't lease Big Four until 1930, the Vanderbilts had been firmly in control of Big Four since at least 1889, thus its operations were dovetailed with NYC(&HR). Big Four was a bonanza of new, lucrative routes for Central, notably Cleveland-Columbus-Cincinnati, Cleveland-Indianapolis-St. Louis, Cincinnati-Indianapolis-Chicago, and Springfield, Ohio-Indianapolis-Peoria, Illinois (as the Peoria & Eastern).

Other important NYC subsidiaries included the Pittsburgh-Youngstown (Ohio) Pittsburgh

& Lake Erie Railroad and the Indiana Harbor Belt Railroad. P&LE gave NYC access to Pittsburgh, a city otherwise heavily influenced by the Pennsylvania Railroad. The IHB was jointly owned with Milwaukee Road and provided NYC with terminal access in Chicago's metropolitan area. NYC also shared ownership, with Canadian Pacific, of the Toronto, Hamilton & Buffalo Railway, which provided a gateway into southern Ontario.

WITH AN ANCHOR IN most major Northeastern and eastern Midwest cities, NYC could hardly do wrong. It carried a tremendous amount of freight and passenger traffic (although overall somewhat less than the Pennsylvania Railroad) up through World War II.

ABOVE: For an Eastern carrier, NYC had relatively low grades throughout its system, but it did sport some hefty steam power. This S-1-class 4-8-4—a "Northern" type on most other roads but called a "Niagara" on the Central—has a good grip on the steep grade (one of the few on NYC's New York-Chicago "Water Level Route") at West Albany, New York, with the westbound *Mohawk* in May 1948.—WILLIAM D. MIDDLETON.

The *20th Century Limited* was considered by many railroad historians to be the ultimate passenger train. From 1902 to 1967, the *Century* sped passengers the 961 miles between America's two largest cities (along with rival Pennsylvania's *Broadway Limited*) in as little as 15½ hours including passenger and train-servicing stops and the restricting speeds of terminal trackage. There is little argument that the train reached its peak in 1938 when new streamlined locomotives and rolling stock were introduced. The '38 *Century* was perhaps the crowning achievement of industrial designer Henry Dreyfuss, who styled the train throughout, from the Roman helmet brow of its streamlined Hudson locomotives (BELOW, leaving Englewood, Illinois, with the *Century* circa 1945) to the train's "Cafe Century" dining cars to the crockery within. RIGHT: A magazine ad illustrates how a red carpet was rolled out for passengers boarding the *Century* at New York and Chicago.—AD, COLLECTION OF C. W. NEWTON; PHOTO COLLECTION OF JAY WILLIAMS.

Central was known for its fast, quality passenger trains, the crowning flagship being the *20th Century Limited*, arguably the world's finest and most-famous passenger train. Launched in 1902, the all-sleeping-car *Century* brought high-class, high-speed overnight service between the nation's two largest cities. When streamlined in 1938, the *20th Century Limited* brought the Art Deco movement to new levels of esteem. During the 16-hour New York-Chicago trip, travelers sipped cocktails at 100 mph on Central's glass-smooth Water Level Route and could avail themselves of the *Century*'s on-board train secretary who could even make theater reservations at New York or Chicago for passengers traveling en route. During its golden age, the *Century* epitomized high society, and reportedly there was a time when only those who were somebody (or knew somebody) could reserve space on the *Century*.

"Home" for most NYC passenger trains, intercity and commuter, was Grand Central

Terminal in midtown Manhattan. Opened in 1913, the 48-track depot to this day remains one of New York City's most-impressive and beloved landmarks. Often mistakenly referred to as Grand Central *Station*, which is actually the designation of the post office within the terminal, GCT's notable attributes include the famous brass clock at the information kiosk at the center of the concourse, and a replica of the northern hemisphere constellation on the concourse ceiling, complete with twinkling "stars." Thank the Vanderbilt family for this ultimate tribute to New York Central and the rail transportation industry. The depot no longer serves intercity passenger trains, but it does remain an important terminal for Manhattan commuters.

LIKE COMPETITOR PENNSY, Central's contribution to the war effort during the early 1940's was immeasurable. But also like the Pennsy (and most other major U.S. railroads), NYC had

been disillusioned by the boom in wartime traffic. Despite the expected downturn from temporary postwar highs in traffic levels, post-World War II euphoria suggested that freight and passenger rail traffic would at least be overall higher than prewar levels. Instead, they fell below, with much traffic diverted to new federally funded highways and emerging air systems.

This disillusionment didn't begin right away. In the heady years immediately following the war, Central took delivery of 780 new lightweight passenger cars—$100 million worth—the largest amount ever ordered then or since. The cars were used to re-equip principal trains, including the *Century*.

Freight service was also upgraded. In 1946, Central introduced its high-speed *Pacemaker* freights. The two trains, one out of Boston and the other out of New York City, ran overnight to Buffalo. Whereas nearly all freight traffic on

Text continued on page 121

ABOVE: At the opposite end of the spectrum from the famous *20th Century Limited* were New York Central's hundreds of daily suburban and local trains, one of which is shown departing North White Plains, New York, for Grand Central Terminal. NYC was a key player in feeding thousands of commuters to Manhattan each weekday morning, returning them home each evening to dozens of communities along two principal routes north out of Manhattan—the Hudson Line along that river to Poughkeepsie and the Harlem Line to Brewster—and one along the west shore of the Hudson north from Weehawken, New Jersey, across the river from New York City. NYC also operated suburban service at Boston and a very modest commuter operation out of Chicago.—MIKE SCHAFER.

RIGHT: The glistening stainless steel parlor-observation lounge car of the *Pacemaker* provides a stark contrast to the gritty surroundings of New York City as the New York-Chicago train makes its suburban stop at 125th Street. BELOW: Further illustrating NYC's intricate ties to metropolitan New York City is this 1964 scene of the New York Central waterfront freight terminal at Weehawken, New Jersey. A switch engine rousts about with a string of refrigerator cars. At the piers just beyond, freight is transferred from freight cars to barges which will be floated to other freight terminals on the opposite shore of the Hudson River (background, with Manhattan as a backdrop), or freight destined for export will be loaded on ships. FACING PAGE: In a serene setting that belies its relative proximity to the wilds of New York City, a westbound New York-Albany local train skims the east shore of the Hudson River near Manitou, New York, in July 1963. The Bear Mountain Bridge looms in the background.—ALL PHOTOS, RICHARD J. SOLOMON.

LEFT: Part of Central's success could be attributed to the fact that it, like competitor Pennsylvania Railroad, served most major industrial centers in the Midwest and Northeast. Train 355, the *Michigan* bound for Chicago, slips out of Detroit in May 1964. The tall building in the background is the depot of NYC subsidiary Michigan Central and NYC's headquarters in the "Motor City."—HANK GOERKE. BELOW: NYC had a strong presence in Ohio. In 1964, a freight rumbles above a main artery (complete with electric trolley buses) in the city of Columbus.—ROGER PUTA, COLLECTION OF MEL FINZER.

Central's four-track main line across New York State was relegated to 45 mph speeds on track Nos. 3 and 4, the *Pacemaker*s were permitted to use the tracks normally assigned to the passenger trains, tracks 1 and 2, and could move at speeds up to 60 mph.

Under new NYC President Alfred Perlman, the railroad in the mid-1950's began an aggressive upgrade by modernizing traffic-control systems, fully dieselizing its fleet of steam (and in some cases electric) locomotives, and embarking on new, strategic freight marketing concepts. One of these was a freight-car innovation known as Flexi-Van, which debuted in 1958. Flexi-Van service represented one of the earliest successful applications of container-on-flatcar (COFC) freight movement in U.S. railroading. Considering that the majority of merchandise freight today moves in containers, Central was ahead of the times. Indeed, Flexi-Van service caught on

well on the NYC, prompting Central to introduce *SuperVan* trains—high-speed Flexi-Van-only trains linking New York and Boston with Chicago, Detroit, St. Louis, and Cincinnati. By 1968, there were 22 scheduled *SuperVan* trains and NYC was running the largest container service in the world. Central's newest diesels were assigned to the *SuperVans*, which were permitted to travel at speeds in excess of 70 mph.

Unfortunately, the times weren't so exciting for NYC passenger trains, and gradually Central's long-distance passenger-train network was largely dismantled. Indicative of these drastic measures was the sudden discontinuance of the *20th Century Limited* in 1967.

But by this time, another unthinkable event was already underway. In 1957, New York Central had announced that it was exploring merger possibilities with one-time foe Pennsylvania Railroad. In the U.S. rail industry of

ABOVE: NYC's westernmost reach brought the railroad into Missouri. Central's main route to St. Louis came out of Cleveland and made a more or less straight shot southwesterly to the Gateway City via Indianapolis and Terre Haute, Indiana, two other important Midwestern interchange points and industrial centers. At St. Louis on a summer day in 1966 a four-unit set of General Motor's Electro-Motive F-type locomotives eases to a halt at the Missouri Pacific yard opposite St. Louis Union Station (out of photo at left) with a jointly operate run-through freight. The train has bypassed Central's own yard on the other side of the Mississippi River in Illinois, and MP will forward it to Texas.—MIKE SCHAFER.

BELOW: NYC 4-6-2 No. 4925 is putting on quite a show for commuters awaiting their Illinois Central suburban train at 51st Street on Chicago's south side on the afternoon of August 4, 1946. The train is a Michigan Central run, possibly the *Wolverine*, en route from IC's Central Station in Chicago to New York via Detroit. Although NYC's main Chicago passenger facility was La Salle Street Station, a lease agreement kept some NYC trains as tenants at IC's Chicago terminal until 1971.—PAUL SLAGER, COLLECTION OF MIKE SCHAFER.

that period, this was considered one of the signs of the Apocalypse. Yet, on February 1, 1968, NYC and PRR joined rails in matrimony, emerging as Penn Central Transportation Company. At the time, NYC had become fairly profitable while PRR was borderline profitable at best, though neither faced long-term financial stability as independent carriers. Nonetheless, by the end of the decade, PC wound up in ruins, a victim of gross mismanagement and a "Red Team" (PRR) versus "Green Team" (NYC) internal rivalry that would not be put to rest.

Nonetheless, Central's spirit and strengths survive in end-of-century America, largely as important arteries of PC successor Conrail. Conrail's former NYC main line between Chicago and Buffalo is one of the busiest in the nation, and Amtrak passenger trains still cruise along the Water Level Route—in some places at speeds in excess of 100 mph, such as west of Albany along a portion of what originally was the old Mohawk & Hudson Rail Road, genesis of the mighty New York Central over 165 years ago.

ABOVE: A westbound freight smokes along NYC's double-track main line at Vickers, Ohio, in May 1962 behind a set of "Sharknose" freight diesels built by Baldwin Locomotive Works.—EMERY GULASH. LEFT: Basking in the glow of morning sun at Englewood station on Chicago's south side on a winter morning early in 1967, the *20th Century Limited* enters the last lap of its trip from New York City into La Salle Street Station. Once one of the most optimistic railroads in terms of providing passenger service, NYC by this time had become thoroughly disillusioned by the passenger train. On December 3, 1967, with almost no warning and little fanfare, the railroad discontinued the *Century*, replacing it with a nameless overnight Chicago-New York/Boston run, which in essence (and with some irony) survives today as Amtrak's popular *Lake Shore Limited*.—JIM BOYD.

THE STANDARD RAILROAD OF THE WORLD

Pennsylvania Railroad

ortune Magazine once referred to the Pennsylvania Railroad as "a nation unto itself." Evidence to back that statement was staggering. At its peak, the "Pennsy" had some 28,000 miles of track, directly serving nearly half of the U.S. population. The railroad owned its own foundries, erecting shops, coal mines, power plants, grain elevators, machine shops, hotels, boats, and a telephone and telegraph system. All this was aside from what you would expect a railroad to own: tracks, locomotives, freight and passenger cars, much land and an impressive array of station facilities, including the likes of 30th Street in Philadelphia and the late, lamented Pennsylvania Station in New York City. In terms of its astronomical assets and ongoing revenue/liability cash flow, the PRR was in fact larger than some countries.

With lines that reached into virtually every major city of the Northeast and eastern Midwest, small wonder that the Pennsy was until after World War II the dominate force—and a keystone, if you will—in American transportation.

Like most other large railroads, the PRR had a modest beginning as a single line; PRR's was through central Pennsylvania connecting Philadelphia with Pittsburgh. As a transportation artery, the first operation between these two cities was not entirely rail, but a state-owned combination of rail, canal and portage railroad—the portage section being a series of ten cable-operated incline railways that carried canal boats over the crest of the Alleghenies between Hollidaysburg and Johnstown. By 1834, this "Main Line of Public Works," from which PRR later derived the nickname for its track across the state (the Main Line), was operating as a through route for freight and passenger transport.

Shortly thereafter it became apparent that an all-rail route between Philadelphia and Pittsburgh would be far more practical, and in 1846 the Pennsylvania Railroad was char-

ISSUED JANUARY 25, 1953

PENNSYLVANIA RAILROAD

FORM 1

tered to build it, much to the chagrin of an older railroad that wished to do the same—the Baltimore & Ohio. This new PRR route chose to follow rivers—in this case the Susquehanna and Juniata—from Harrisburg to Altoona to maintain moderate grades. At first, PRR handled the challenge of surmounting the Allegheny ridge just beyond Altoona by utilizing part of the Portage Railroad incline system, but this was temporary. In 1854 the PRR opened a new route over the mountain which included the now-famous Horseshoe Curve and a tunnel under the summit. Now there was a truly continuous all-rail route between what were destined to become Pennsylvania's two largest and most-important cities.

Much of PRR's growth was achieved through lease or purchase of numerous smaller railroads, lines like the Pittsburgh, Fort Wayne & Chicago through whose 1869 lease the Pennsy arrived in Chicago. At about the same time, leases of various properties in New Jersey brought the PRR to Jersey City on the fringe of a rapidly growing port and city, New York. By 1873, similar expansion south of Philadelphia extended PRR to Washington (again to the chagrin of B&O, which already operated a thriving route into Washington). West of Pittsburgh and south of the above-mentioned PFtW&C during the mid-19th Century, a gaggle of little railroads were themselves consolidating with other lines, with PRR—as a potentially important traffic generator for these lines—shepherding the activity. Many of these lines wound up as part of the new (in 1890) Pittsburgh, Cincinnati, Chicago & St. Louis Railway, a line heavily influenced by PRR interests and in 1921 leased to PRR after further consolidation. Now the Pennsylvania Railroad empire reached St. Louis, gateway to the West, at the same time tapping such important cities as Columbus and Cincinnati, Ohio, Louisville, Kentucky, and Indianapolis, Indiana.

PRR's purchase of the Long Island Rail

FACING PAGE: Pennsylvania Railroad's heroic nature is embodied in this 1960s scene at Horseshoe Curve of a westbound freight tackling the climb to the summit of the Allegheny Mountains. The "Pennsy" was one of the most revered railroads in North America, if not the world, during the first half of the 20th Century. FACING PAGE INSET: Unique to the PRR and some of its subsidiary railroads were its position-light signals, thousands of which safely guided the movement of Pennsy trains throughout the system. Whereas most railroads relied on signals which used color aspects (red, green, yellow, etc.) to indicate track and block conditions, PRR's position-light signals featured rows of fog-piercing yellow lights whose position—horizontal, vertical, diagonal—rather than color dictated train movement. This lonely signal stood guard on PRR's old Pittsburgh, Fort Wayne & Chicago main line, route of the *Broadway Limited*.—TWO PHOTOS, MIKE SCHAFER. LEFT: PRR's timetable from January 1953 featured a painting of Horseshoe Curve by noted artist Grif Teller.

PENNSYLVANIA RAILROAD AT A GLANCE

Headquarters: Philadelphia, Pennsylvania

Mileage
1950: 10,000
1962: 9,756

Locomotives owned as of 1963:
Diesel: 2,402   Electric: 254

Rolling stock owned as of 1963:
Freight cars: 139,356   Passenger: 3,546

Principal routes as of 1950:
Philadelphia-Harrisburg-Pittsburgh, Pa.
New York-Washington, D.C.
Pittsburgh-Fort Wayne, Ind.-Chicago
Pittsburgh-Indianapolis, Ind.-St. Louis, Mo.
Pittsburgh-Cleveland, Ohio
Baltimore, Md.-Buffalo, N.Y.
Wilmington, Del.-Norfolk, Va.
Chicago-Columbus, Ohio
Logansport, Ind.-Louisville, Ky.
Logansport-Cincinnati
Fort Wayne, Ind.-Mackinaw City, Mich.
Columbus-Toledo, Ohio-Detroit, Mich.

Notable passenger trains (listed alphabetically)
Broadway Limited (New York-Chicago)
Clevelander (New York-Cleveland)
Cincinnati Limited (New York-Cincinnati)
Colonial (Boston-Washington, joint with New Haven)
Congressional (New York-Washington)
Duquesne (New York-Pittsburgh)
Edison (New York-Washington)
The *General* (New York-Chicago)
Golden Triangle (Chicago-Pittsburgh)
Jeffersonian (New York-St. Louis)
Kentuckian (Chicago-Louisville)
Liberty Limited (Washington-Chicago)
Manhattan Limited (New York/Washington-Chicago)
Pennsylvania Limited (New York/Washington-Chicago)
Penn Texas (New York-Washington-St. Louis)
Pittsburgher (New York-Pittsburgh)
Red Arrow (New York-Detroit)
St. Louisan (New York/Washington-St. Louis)
Senator (Boston-Washington, joint with New Haven)
"Spirit of St. Louis" (New York-St. Louis)
South Wind (Chicago-Miami, joint with L&N, ACL and Florida East Coast)
Trail Blazer (New York-Chicago)
Union (Chicago-Columbus)
The PRR was also a forwarder for several other connecting railroads' passenger trains to major on-line PRR cities, principally in the New York-Florida market.

Road in 1900 prompted PRR to devise a plan to "invade" Manhattan, where the also-expanding New York Central—already the arch rival of PRR—held strong through an impressive terminal complex known as Grand Central. In 1904, PRR began construction on its own Manhattan station complex. The project included two approach tunnels under the Hudson River, four under the East River (for Long Island trains) and a main line between the Hudson tunnels and the PRR's existing Jersey City-Washington main. For reasons of safety and and to reduce the hazards of asphyxiation in a confined area, the whole complex was electrified. In 1910, the project was completed and Pennsylvania Station—which some would call PRR's monument to itself—opened to the public.

During the first half of the 20th Century, Pennsy achieved its almost-legendary status as the "Standard Railroad of the World," and

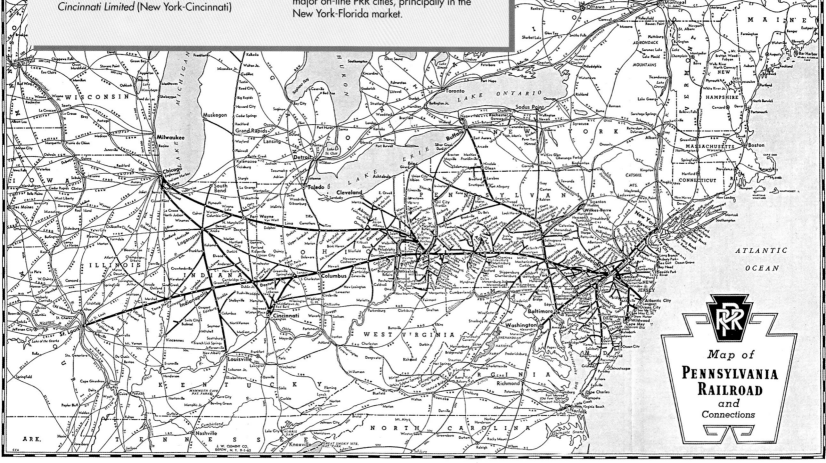

Map of
PENNSYLVANIA RAILROAD
and
Connections

was a powerful player in American business—and not just railroading. So influential was Pennsy to matters regarding its home state that the railroad's lobbyist to the state government was often referred to as Pennsylvania's "51st senator." At one time or another, Pennsy also had controlling interests in other major—and sometimes competing—railroads, such as B&O, Norfolk & Western, Chesapeake & Ohio, New Haven, and Boston & Maine. This influence also extended to a number of subsidiary or otherwise affiliated railroads, notably the New York & Long Branch (jointly owned with Central Railroad Company of New Jersey); Lehigh Valley; Detroit, Toledo & Ironton; Ann Arbor; Pennsylvania-Reading Seashore Lines (jointly owned with Reading Company); and the Wabash.

Actually, in the context of U.S. railroads, PRR was anything but standard, with a vast array of locomotives and rolling stock that bore a look that was uniquely Pennsy. The "standard" reference was to itself. Unlike most other U.S. railroads, which relied heavily on independent locomotive- and car-building companies, PRR designed many of its locomotives, passenger cars, freight cars, signaling systems and stations in-house to specifications and standards which themselves were quite different from those followed by most railroads. PRR even built a significant number of its locomotives and cars at its own shop facilities, and when outside firms were hired to construct equipment, they had to follow PRR specs.

Pennsy's most famous shop complex was

ABOVE: "Home" for the Pennsylvania Railroad was Philadelphia, also home for the annual Army/Navy football game. This event draws a tremendous number of people to the Philadelphia area, and in earlier days thousands of them arrived aboard chartered trains. Two of those trains for the 1964 game are shown at the game-train staging area in Philadelphia. A General Motors Electro-Motive Division (EMD) passenger diesel, model E8, clad in PRR's familiar tuscan red livery, shares the limelight (and sunlight) with one of Pennsy's most distinguished locomotive types, a GG1 electric. The "G's", as they were sometimes called, were introduced in 1935 and remained in service long after the PRR ceased to exist in 1968, hauling trains for Amtrak well into the 1980's.—JOHN DZIOBKO.

TOP: Steam-era Pennsy operated a vast fleet of passenger trains, which required an equally vast battalion of passenger steam power. The dominant (and ubiquitous) locomotive in this category were PRR's K4-class Pacifics (4-6-2's), one of which steps out of Dayton, Ohio, with the Columbus section of the Chicago-bound *Union*. Date: July 21, 1951.—R. D. ACTON SR. ABOVE: The marshalling of millions of freight cars was often handled by 0-6-0 switchers of the B-6 class, such as the 5261 at Camden, New Jersey, in 1956.—JOHN DZIOBKO.

Altoona Works. Virtually a city in itself, Altoona Works was created by the Pennsylvania Railroad in 1849 when it established a site for a yard and shop complex at the base of the climb over the Allegheny summit. From these modest beginnings grew a world-class shop complex as well as a respectable city, whose population today exceeds 50,000 inhabitants. Altoona Works comprised Juniata Shops, Altoona Car Shops, Altoona Machine Shops and South Altoona Foundries. Altoona Works turned out its first locomotive

in 1866, and large numbers of PRR steam (and electric) locomotives were built there from that time on, as were countless freight and passenger cars. (In recent years, successor Conrail even assembled Electro-Motive Division diesels at Altoona.)

The brawny steam locomotives outshopped by Altoona and other companies were distinctive, reliable and sometimes record-breaking. PRR's S1-class locomotive of 1939, for example, with its unusual 6-4-4-6 wheel arrangement (six pilot wheels, two sets of four drivers, and six trailing wheels), was at the time the world's largest and fastest coal-burning locomotive. It could pull a 1,200-ton train at a steady 100 mph on straight track. Curves and switches were the downfall of this long, rigid locomotive, which was not duplicated. Far more successful were PRR's Class K4 Pacific-type locomotives (4-6-2 wheel arrangement, common on railroads throughout the U.S.) of which 350 were built at Altoona and 75 at Baldwin Locomotives Works.

One of Pennsy's most-notable and most-important 20th Century improvements was its program of electrification; that is, the conversion of train propulsion from steam to electric

on selected routes. In a sense, the program began by default with the construction of Pennsylvania Station in New York City. With much of the approach and terminal trackage underground, steam power was impractical and polluting, and it had been outlawed by the City of New York. (These same statutes would later apply to diesel power, so trains in and out of today's Penn Station, on the site of the original Pennsylvania Station are all still electric powered.)

In 1915, PRR electrified its "Main Line" route west from Philadelphia to Paoli. In 1928

Text continued on page 132

TOP AND ABOVE: Among Pennsy's awesome army of freight steam locomotives were some 500 Decapod-type engines (2-10-0's) built principally by Baldwin Locomotive Works—to PRR specifications, of course. Designated as Class I-1's, no fewer than four of them here move a 105-car, 9,580-ton freight upgrade on PRR's Sunbury-Mt. Carmel branch in southeastern Pennsylvania on a May morning in 1952. Two I-1's are up front while two shove on the hind end.—PHOTOGRAPHER UNKNOWN. LEFT: A more quaint side of Pennsy is evident in this street scene at Burlington, New Jersey, on March 27, 1954. Engine 518, a K4 Pacific, slices through downtown with the *Nelly Bly*, bound from New York to Atlantic City.—JOHN DZIOBKO.

From 1902 to 1995, the *Broadway Limited* was an institution in New York-Chicago rail transportation. The overnight speedster was Pennsy' top-of-the-line train, its all-private-room accommodations serving an elite clientele who sipped Manhattans in the train's bar-lounge observation car and dined on Roast Duck a la Orange in the twin-unit diner. TOP: Still shiny, clean and all-Pullman in July 1967, the *Broadway* makes a grand exit from Chicago.— MIKE SCHAFER. ABOVE: *Broadway* gate sign at Harrisburg, Pennsylvania, 1967.—ROGER PUTA, COLLECTION OF MEL FINZER. RIGHT: Nether rain nor sleet . . . the *Broadway* heads out Englewood, Illinois, for New York City on a rainy June evening in 1966.—RON LUNDSTROM.

130

ABOVE: Pennsy was one of a small group of roads that tested one of General Motors' two experimental lightweight *Aerotrains*, which essentially were but standard bus bodies (from GM's motor coach division) on flanged wheels, powered by an Electro-Motive LWT-12 locomotive. As with numerous other lightweight-train concepts of the period, the idea was to reduce the costs of passenger-train operation while making rail travel more attractive. PRR named its test set the *Pennsy Aerotrain* and ran it on a day schedule between Philadelphia and Pittsburgh. It is shown westbound crossing the Susquehanna River on Rockville Bridge—the longest stone-arch rail bridge in North America—near Harrisburg, Pennsylvania, on March 25, 1956. Apparently PRR was not impressed with the futuristic train, for the railroad never ordered its own *Aerotrains*. The set shown and its twin sister ultimately wound up on in commuter service on the Rock Island (see page 73).—JOHN DZIOBKO.

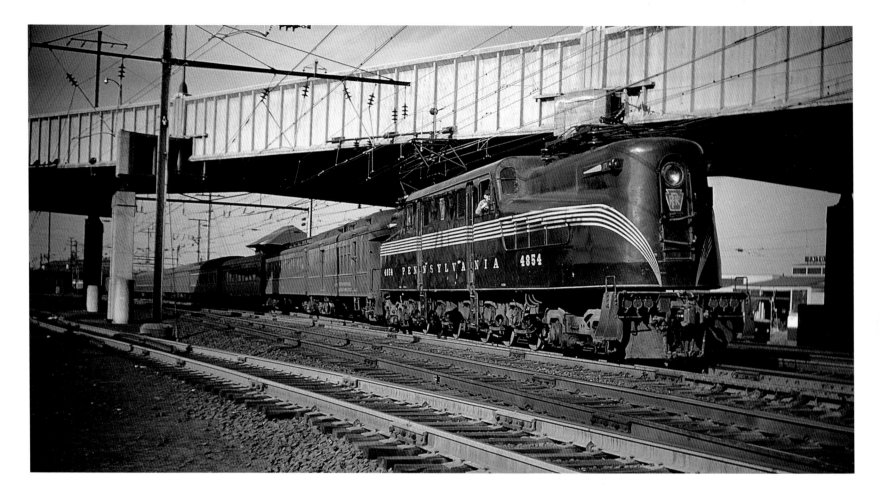

Pennsy embraced electrification in a big way: Nearly 670 of its route-miles—2,260 track-miles when yard and terminal tracks were included—were electrified, making PRR's the most-extensive application of electrification in North American railroading. King of the catenary (the overhead wires that feed the power to the locomotives) were the remarkable GG1 locomotives, at home in both freight and passenger service. ABOVE: Wearing PRR's hallowed "pinstripe" scheme, GG1 4854 brings Lehigh Valley Railroad's *Maple Leaf* past Hunter Tower near Newark, New Jersey, on May 19, 1955. LV's passenger trains terminated in Manhattan and were ushered into Pennsylvania Station by PRR electric locomotives. RIGHT: The success of the GG1's spelled the demise of many older electric freight motors, although a few continued in limited freight and pusher service well into the 1960s. Here a Class P-5a electric boxcab helps push a freight uphill at Columbia, Pennsylvania, in the summer of 1964.—BOTH PHOTOS, JOHN DZIOBKO.

the main line between Philly and Washington was electrified as far as Wilmington, Delaware. By 1933, electrification had been extended north from Philadelphia to Manhattan Transfer, New Jersey (near Newark), where the already electrified route out of Pennsylvania Station and under the Hudson River ended. In 1935, the overhead wires reached Washington, D.C., and in 1938 Paoli to Harrisburg was electrified. Initially, simple but powerful box-cab electric locomotives handled many of the train assignments on the newly energized routes (electrified commuter trains comprised electric-motored passenger cars rather than being locomotive-hauled). In 1935 a new breed of electric locomotive—one

destined to make the history books—made its debut: the famous GG1. Riding on a maze of wheels, the streamstyled dual-direction "G's" effortlessly hummed along, moving passenger and freight trains at high speed between Harrisburg, Philadelphia, Washington and New York for nearly the next half century.

Pride of the Pennsy was the all-sleeping-car *Broadway Limited*, one of the finest passenger trains in North America. Originally named *Pennsylvania Special*, the posh train began New York-Chicago service in 1902. It was streamlined in 1938 (on the same date as its arch competitor, New York Central's *20th Century Limited*) with cars equipped with a variety of private rooms, modern lounges and dining

BELOW: Twin Electro-Motive FP7 passenger diesels invade the streets of Sunbury, Pennsylvania, with the eastbound *Washington Express* on a bright but chilly spring afternoon in March 1956. Though PRR was better known for big-name trains like the *Broadway Limited*, *"Spirit of St. Louis"*, and the *Congressional*, this run was a perfect example of how PRR also provided at least a basic passenger service to just about every nook and cranny of its system. As is also evident in this view, PRR moved a wealth of mail and express, which is what really paid the bills on such secondary passenger runs.—JOHN DZIOBKO.

ABOVE: Missouri was as far west as PRR's sprawl reached. On August 4, 1966, the *Penn Texas* embarks on its 1,050-mile journey from St. Louis Union Station to New York City. The train's name alluded to a time when it carried through sleeping cars from Dallas, San Antonio, El Paso and Houston, all handled to St. Louis on Missouri Pacific and Frisco trains. At St. Louis, these through cars were switched on to the *Penn Texas*, thereby providing single-seat (or bed, as the case may be) service from Texas to the East Coast. By the time of this photo, the through cars were gone, but passengers could still make a walking connection between MP's *Texas Eagle* and the *Penn Texas*.—MIKE SCHAFER.

area, and a barber shop and valet. The train covered the 907.7 miles separating New York and Chicago in 16 hours (for a time, 15½ hours eastbound), or nearly a mile a minute average speed including stops and a trip over the Allegheny Mountains. The *Broadway* turned out to be one of the last passenger trains in the U.S. to boast "All-Pullman" (sleeping-car) service, a status it lost in 1967. The tarnished remnant of this once-noble PRR train was discontinued on September 10, 1995, by Amtrak, which had inherited the *Broadway* 24 years earlier.

Although the PRR has been called a nation unto itself, when it came to World War II, the

Pennsylvania Railroad was a pillar of patriotism to the U.S. Mustering nearly every piece of locomotive and rolling stock it owned, PRR moved double the freight traffic and four times the passenger traffic that it had been moving prior to Pearl Harbor Day.

The war was kind to U.S. railroads only in terms of cash flow. After the staggering war effort, railroads—including the seemingly indestructible PRR—found themselves saddled with war-worn equipment and infrastructure. Complicating the matter was the expected postwar decline in traffic; not expected was the fact that the decline sometimes dropped below what had been normal traffic

Pennsy operated a vast array of suburban and local services, particularly around metropolitan New York City and Philadelphia. TOP: On PRR's electrified Main Line route west from Philadelphia, a two-car electric suburban train skims through Radnor, Pennsylvania, en route to Paoli on April 12, 1964.—WILLIAM D. MIDDLETON. ABOVE: Suburban trains served their own (aptly named) depot in downtown Philadelphia.—MIKE SCHAFER. LEFT: PRR served some local lines with motorcars, such as this one pulling a conventional coach on a Camden-Trenton (New Jersey) run in the fall of 1964.—JOHN DZIOBKO.

levels prior to the war, leaving railroads strapped for monies necessary for recapitalization and rebuilding. Further, the government turned its back on the railroads, opting instead to invest in highway and air infrastructure.

PRR nonetheless soldiered forward into a new postwar era, concentrating mainly on dieselization of its massive locomotive fleet. However, little other modernization and route rationalization (i.e., abandonments) occurred. As freight and passenger traffic was diverted to new federal- and state-funded highways, interstates and airports, what had for decades been a seemingly effortless task for PRR—survival—now became a critical war of its own.

The Pennsylvania Railroad both won and lost that war. In 1957 PRR announced its intention to merge with its greatest rival, the New York Central, which had experienced many of the same postwar problems as had PRR and other major carriers. On February 1, 1968, the PRR-NYC merger was consummated, and Penn Central was born. NYC entered the merger as a profitable carrier; the PRR was less financially stable but holding its own. Penn Central proved that two rights didn't necessarily make an even bigger, better right. The new railroad quickly unraveled, caught in a quagmire of managerial problems. Penn Central went bust on June 21, 1970, becoming the largest U.S. corporation ever to go bankrupt up to that time.

The Pennsylvania Railroad still exists in the sense that some of its components survive today as strategic elements in a newly invigorated U.S. rail transportation network. Heavy freight trains still struggle up and around Horseshoe Curve, but today they are hoisted by the blue diesels of the profitable Conrail system. Those same Conrail diesels still move product and produce in and out of Chicago, Philadelphia, Pittsburgh and St. Louis, though most of the old PRR west of Pittsburgh has been abandoned or sold, save for the mainline west of Terre Haute to St. Louis. Meanwhile, Amtrak's electric-powered *Metroliner*s dash along with thousands of passengers daily at speeds of 125 mph over the old Pennsy main line between New York City and the nation's capital.

With all this in mind, the Pennsy in a sense did win its final war.

FACING PAGE: Pittsburgh-bound, two diesels grind up the four-track main line around Horseshoe Curve with a freight.—MIKE SCHAFER. ABOVE: A peeled keystone emblem on the nose of the locomotive leading Cincinnati-Chicago train 71 into Chicago's suburban Englewood station in 1966 symbolizes the waning years of the late, great Pennsylvania Railroad.—RON LUNDSTROM.

THE FRIENDLY SOUTHERN PACIFIC

Southern Pacific

enerable Southern Pacific is a California institution, right down to its prestigious address: One Market Plaza, San Francisco. In fact, the SP—or "Espee" as it is sometimes known among rail historians—has probably starred as a prop in more Hollywood movies than any other American railroad. (When Bing Crosby and Danny Kaye alight from the train at "Pine Tree, Vermont" in the 1954 classic "White Christmas," they're actually detraining from SP equipment at a decidedly California location.)

End to end, as measured along its main trunk routes, SP is the longest old-line railroad in the U.S. If in 1955 you were to board SP's *Shasta Daylight* at Portland, Oregon, on a Friday morning, transfer to the *Coast Daylight* at San Francisco Saturday morning, and then to the *Sunset Limited* at Los Angeles Saturday evening, you would pull into New Orleans on Monday afternoon—and still be on the Southern Pacific Lines, 3,656 miles from where you started. In terms of operating revenues, SP was overshadowed only by the New York Central and Pennsylvania Railroads.

SP's early history and development is quite complex and involved the acquisition of numerous railroads initially independent of SP as well as the creation of subsidiary railroads by SP (or predecessor Central Pacific) interests for purposes of construction or tax advantages. More than most other railroads, SP maintained a dizzying array of "paper" railroads interlinked through stock ownership and complex lease agreements, some of which exist to this day.

The genesis of SP can be traced to a major event—the admission of California as a state in 1850—and to four individuals: Collis P. Huntington, Charles Crocker, Mark Hopkins and Leland Stanford. These Sacramento businessmen, known as the "Big Four" (no relation to the New York Central subsidiary of that name), financed what became the Central

Pacific Railroad with the generous assistance of the federal government. The CP would fulfill California's dream of being connected to the East by building east from the Sacramento area into Nevada and Utah to meet another fledgling railroad—the Union Pacific—building west from Omaha. CP's first locomotive entered service in 1863, and on May 10, 1869, CP and UP met at Promontory, Utah (near Ogden) creating the first transcontinental rail route.

The CP line to Ogden crossed California's rugged Sierra Range via Donner Pass, made famous by the ill-fated Donner party expedition, which had become stranded in one of the Sierra's famous snowstorms. The Sacramento-Ogden line became known as Southern Pacific's Overland Route.

Even before the Golden Spike ceremony at Promontory, CP had begun pushing west from Sacramento into the San Francisco Bay area with two different lines, one built and one purchased. The San Francisco & San Jose Railroad opened its route between those two cities down the San Francisco Peninsula in 1864. From San Jose, the original Southern Pacific—now controlled by the Big Four—aimed its rails southeast through the San Joaquin Valley toward Arizona.

CP in 1870 purchased the California & Oregon and the San Joaquin Valley Railroad, thus extending itself both north and south from Sacramento. By 1874, CP and SP had extended the Valley route all the way through the San Joaquin Valley to Bakersfield.

SP's goal was to head to Southern California and turn east to meet a railroad building out of New Orleans. This it did, but only after a detour through the growing port of Los Angeles. SP reached Los Angeles in 1876 by building east from Bakersfield over the Tehachapi Mountains, a feat which involved the construction of a loop (Tehachapi Loop) to gain elevation in a limited area. Upon reaching Los Angeles, SP linked up with existing trackage to

FACING PAGE: The classic Southern Pacific of yore has come to life once again at the California State Railroad Museum in Sacramento on a starry spring night in 1984. Former SP restored "Daylight" 4-8-4 No. 4449 (now owned by the City of Portland, Oregon), en route from Portland to New Orleans with the *Louisiana World's Fair Daylight*, stands symbolic of Espee's proud past during the exposition train's layover at Sacramento. Joining in the festivities is the museum's restored *Daylight* diesel 6051 (right in photo).—MIKE SCHAFER/JIM BOYD/JOHN GIESKE. FACING PAGE INSET: The nose of an Electro-Motive (GM) freight diesel at Medford, Oregon, in 1990 reveals a decidedly SP trait: plenty of headlights and warning lights.—BRIAN SOLOMON. LEFT: An SP timetable from 1932 displays the railroad's time-honored tracks-into-the-sunset logo, still in use in the late 1990's.

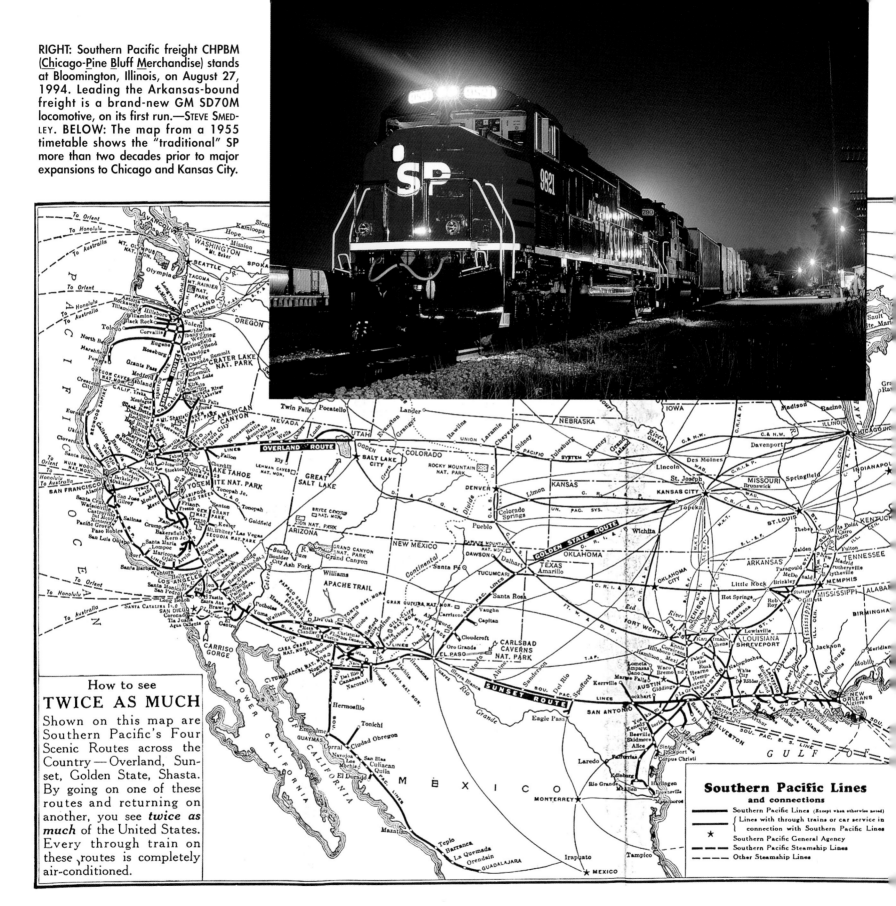

RIGHT: Southern Pacific freight CHPBM (Chicago-Pine Bluff Merchandise) stands at Bloomington, Illinois, on August 27, 1994. Leading the Arkansas-bound freight is a brand-new GM SD70M locomotive, on its first run.—STEVE SMEDLEY. BELOW: The map from a 1955 timetable shows the "traditional" SP more than two decades prior to major expansions to Chicago and Kansas City.

How to see
TWICE AS MUCH
Shown on this map are Southern Pacific's Four Scenic Routes across the Country — Overland, Sunset, Golden State, Shasta. By going on one of these routes and returning on another, you see *twice as much* of the United States. Every through train on these routes is completely air-conditioned.

Southern Pacific Lines
and connections

———	Southern Pacific Lines (Except when otherwise noted)
———	Lines with through trains or car service in connection with Southern Pacific Lines
★	Southern Pacific General Agency
– – –	Southern Pacific Steamship Lines
— — —	Other Steamship Lines

Indio, California, and continued east, reaching Yuma, Arizona, in 1877. SP was supposed to connect with the Texas & Pacific at this point, but the financially strapped T&P was stuck in Fort Worth, Texas, over a thousand miles east. SP kept building, reaching Tucson in 1880 and El Paso in 1881. T&P, now under the control of New York financier Jay Gould, was approaching El Paso from the east and complaining that SP had appropriated its right-of-way. In 1881, though, Gould reached an agreement with Huntington, who had become SP's dominate figure, to meet the SP at Sierra Blanca, Texas, and operate T&P trains over SP's line into El Paso, an arrangement that survives to this day.

In 1883 SP met up with the Galveston, Harrisburg & San Antonio Railroad, which Huntington and his associates had purchased in 1879. Another new transcontinental route had opened. From San Francisco to New Orleans, this would become known as SP's Sunset Route.

Also in 1883, SP had built a line east from its Bakersfield-Los Angeles line at Mojave to Needles, California, on the Arizona state line to meet the Atlantic & Pacific, an affiliate of the Santa Fe, working its way west. SP later traded this line to Santa Fe for the latter's line from Nogales, Arizona, into Mexico, giving Santa Fe a major foothold in California.

In 1884 the Southern Pacific Company was chartered (in Kentucky, no less) to lease the myriad of companies that formed the Central Pacific and Southern Pacific system; SP eventually leased CP in 1923.

The north end of the SP system—what would become the Shasta Route—jelled after the Sunset Route fell into place. Through its California & Oregon Railroad purchased in 1870, SP continued building north from where the C&O had left off (near what is now Chico, California) through Dunsmuir, California, and over the Siskiyou Mountains, reaching Ashland, Oregon, in 1887. There it met—and purchased—the Oregon & California Railroad, which had completed its line between Ashland and Portland in 1884.

By the turn of the century, SP's principal lines were in place, with a couple of notable exceptions. One of SP's best-known routes, the Coast Line between San Jose and Los Angeles via Santa Barbara, was not completed until 1904. The Golden State Route connecting the Chicago, Rock Island & Pacific at Santa Rosa, New Mexico, with SP's Sunset Route at El Paso was completed in 1902 as the El Paso & North Eastern. The EP&NE, built by one Charles R. Eddy, was acquired by the El Paso & Southwestern, the railroad arm of copper producer Phelps Dodge, in 1905. EP&SW operated a competing line between Tucson and El Paso serving Phelps Dodge's properties. The link to the Rock Island gave Phelps Dodge its own line to Eastern markets. Obviously, this situation did not benefit SP, and it bought the EP&SW in 1924.

After the turn of the century, SP came under control of E. H. Harriman, who also controlled Union Pacific. Harriman believed that improving the physical plant of his rail-

SOUTHERN PACIFIC AT A GLANCE

Headquarters: San Francisco, California

Mileage:
1950: 15,039 (including subsidiary St. Louis-Southwestern)
1995: 17,340 (including subsidiaries SSW, SPCSL, and D&RGW)

Locomotive fleet as of 1963:
Diesel: 2,096

Rolling stock as of 1963:
Freight cars: 77,401   Passenger cars: 1,002

Principal lines as of 1950:
Los Angeles-San Francisco via San Jose
San Jose-Ogden, Utah
Davis, Calif.-Portland, Ore., via Chemult and Eugene, Ore.
Eugene-Black Butte via Roseburg, Ore.
Sacramento-Burbank (Los Angeles) via Bakersfield
Lathrop-Martinez, Calif.
Los Angeles-New Orleans via Phoenix, Ariz.
El Paso, Texas-Tucumcari, N. M.
Galveston-Dallas/Denison, Texas, via Houston and Hearne
Rosenburg-Brownsville, Texas
San Antonio-Corpus Christi, Texas
Houston-Shreveport, La.
St. Louis-Dallas/Fort Worth (SSW)
Memphis, Tenn.-Brinkley, Ark.
Mount Pleasant-Waco, Texas (SSW)
Lewisville, Ark.-Shreveport, La. (SSW)

Principal added lines as of 1996:
Tucumcari-St. Louis via Kansas City
St. Louis-Chicago via Bloomington, Ill.
Kansas City-Chicago via Quincy, Ill. (trackage rights on Burlington Northern Santa Fe)
Kansas City-Chicago via Fort Madison, Iowa (track-age rights on Burlington Northern Santa Fe)
Ogden-Pueblo, Colo., via Salt Lake City, Utah, and Salida, Colo.
Dotsero-Pueblo, Colo., via Granby and Denver
Pueblo-Kansas City via Salinas, Kan. (trackage rights on Union Pacific)

Notable passenger trains (listed alphabetically):
Argonaut (Los Angeles-New Orleans)
Cascade (Oakland-Portland)
City of San Francisco (Oakland-Chicago via Ogden; joint with Union Pacific and Chicago & North Western [Milwaukee Road after 1955])
Coast Daylight (San Francisco-Los Angeles via San Luis Obispo; for a time also known as *Morning Daylight*)
Del Monte (San Francisco-Monterey, Calif.)
Golden State Limited (Los Angeles-Chicago via Tucumcari; joint with Rock Island)
Hustler (Houston-Dallas)
Imperial (Los Angeles-Chicago via Tucumcari; joint with Rock Island)
Lark (Oakland/San Francisco-Los Angeles via San Luis Obispo)
Owl (San Francisco-Los Angeles via Bakersfield)
Sacramento Daylight (Sacramento-Los Angeles via Bakersfield)
San Francisco Overland (Until October 1955, Oakland-Chicago via Ogden, joint with UP and C&NW; after 1955 it was an Oakland-St. Louis train joint with the Wabash Railroad)
San Joaquin Daylight (Oakland-Los Angeles via Bakersfield)
Shasta Daylight (Oakland-Portland)
Starlight (San Francisco-Los Angeles)
Sunbeam (Houston-Dallas)
Sunset Limited (Initially San Franciso-New Orleans via San Joaquin Valley; was later cut back to Los Angeles-New Orleans)

TOP: Espee had an impressive array of steam power, and two of the railroad's more well-known types are featured in this scene east of Oxnard, California, in 1953. Daylight 4-8-4 No. 4458 on the point of the eastbound *Coast Daylight* is about to overtake eastbound freight No. 830 led by a Cab-Forward 2-8-8-4.—WILLIAM D. MIDDLETON. ABOVE: It's 1968—well into the waning years of Espee passenger service—but this scene aboard a 1941-built lounge car on the *Del Monte* reflects an era when the railroad welcomed passengers with style and friendly service.—ROBERT P. SCHMIDT.

roads would ensure their business success. Among the most important Harriman-inspired achievements for SP was the construction of the Lucin Cutoff across the Great Salt Lake, shortening SP's Overland route between Ogden and Lucin, Utah, by 44 miles. The Harriman regime also built a new easy-grade route—the Bayshore Cutoff—for traffic in and out of San Francisco.

The 1926 opening of the 278-mile Natron Cutoff—later renamed the Shasta Route—between Eugene and Black Butte, Oregon, significantly altered north-south through-traffic patterns on the Shasta Route overall. The Natron Cutoff had easier grades and thus became the principal route for freight and passenger business between Oregon and California; the original route between Black Butte and Eugene became known as the Siskiyou Line, serving as a local route for lumber traffic.

WELL INTO THE 1950s, SP's fielded an extensive array of highly regarded passenger trains including a successful suburban operation on the San Francisco peninsula. Leader of the intercity fleet was the legendary *Daylight* (later renamed *Morning Daylight* and then *Coast Daylight* to differentiate it from other trains added to the *Daylight* family), the passenger train most often associated with the classic-era Southern Pacific. Inaugurated in 1922 between San Francisco and Los Angeles, the *Daylight Limited* was the first all-SP train to be streamlined, in 1937—after which SP unabashedly called the new *Daylight* "the world's most beautiful train." The million-dollar steam-powered streamliner wore a rousing livery of red, orange and black.

The overnight companion train of the *Daylight*s on the Coast Line was the *Lark*, which had been inaugurated in 1910. By the 1920s the *Lark* had become the train of choice for businessmen and film stars. In 1941 it was re-equipped as a streamliner.

SP's longest run was the *Sunset Limited*, introduced in 1884 between New Orleans and San Francisco. It was cut back to Los Angeles during World War II, and it became a streamliner in 1950. Amtrak assumed operation of the *Sunset Limited* in 1971; as of 1996, the train still operates, making it the oldest continuously operated name train in North America.

Sharing the Sunset Route west of El Paso to Los Angeles were the jointly operated trains of Rock Island and SP over the Golden State route. Chief among them was the *Golden State Limited*, introduced in 1902 between Chicago and Los Angeles. It was streamlined in 1947, but it was the weakest of the well-known Chicago-L.A. transcons—including Santa Fe's *Chief* and *Super Chief* and UP's *City of Los Angeles*—and was discontinued in 1968.

Stars of the Shasta Route were the overnight *Cascade* and the day-run *Shasta Daylight*, both of them Portland-Oakland trains. Interestingly, the spirit of the *Cascade* and the *Coast Daylight* survive today as Amtrak's Seattle-Los Angeles *Coast Starlight*.

On a more national scope, SP's most well-known train was the *City of San Francisco*, a jointly operated (with UP and Chicago & North Western) Chicago-Oakland streamliner launched in 1936 and sharing the Overland Route with other C&NW-UP-SP trains such as the *Forty-Niner*, *Pacific Limited* and *San Francisco Challenger*.

SP'S SWEEPING ARC from the Pacific Northwest to the Gulf of Mexico together with its Over-

ABOVE: Southern Pacific's best-known landmark is Tehachapi Loop, on what is now SP's busiest freight line connecting Northern California with Los Angeles and the Sunset Route; Santa Fe is a tenant on the SP through Tehachapi Loop, which is 77 feet high at the point shown above. What appears to be two trains in this photo is actually one train climbing the loop. Longer trains will cross above themselves, as in this 1969 scene of an eastbound freight. Two mid-train helper locomotives, visible in the foreground, assist the four lead locomotives in the 2.52 percent climb toward the summit of the Tehachapi Mountains.—MIKE SCHAFER.

land leg into the interior provided the railroad with a diverse freight-traffic base: lumber products from Oregon, produce from California's fertile valleys, chemicals from Texas and Louisiana and much import/export traffic through the Bay Area, Los Angeles, Portland, and New Orleans.

The one-time importance of produce traffic to SP was evident in the solid reefer (refrigerator car) trains that once poured out of California, and SP and UP were once partners in a vast concern known as Pacific Fruit Express. SP and UP owned equal shares of this company, which had its own refrigerator-car fleet—more than 22,000 strong as of 1962—for moving fruit, vegetables and other perishables. UP and SP split up the PFE fleet in the 1970's, and though PFE still exists as an SP subsidiary, most of the perishable traffic has since been diverted to trucks.

Moving freight (and sometimes passenger trains) was an ongoing challenge in SP's mountainous territory. The Overland Route's crossing of the Sierra Range—Donner Pass—was particularly brutal account of steep grades and the Sierra's penchant for wicked

ABOVE: The Wasatch Mountains serve as an impressive backdrop to a utilitarian side of Southern Pacific: that of its Ogden (Utah) engine terminal on a spring morning in 1967. The flat-faced Alco passenger diesel in the center has brought in that morning's eastbound *City of San Francisco*, while various Electro-Motive freight units—including one still clad in the road's "black widow" scheme (right in photo)—await westbound freight assignments.—RON LUNDSTROM. BELOW. Espee's Overland Route from Sacramento to Ogden included a trip on the Lucin Cutoff across the Great Salt Lake. On a bright July morning in 1969, 100 years after the last spike was driven at Promontory, Utah, several miles north of this location, the eastbound *City of San Francisco* charges over the lake.—MIKE SCHAFER.

blizzards, one of which in 1952 stranded the *City of San Francisco* for several days near Emigrant Gap in a manner that had spooky parallels to the doomed Donner party more than a century earlier. SP's Donner Pass line is laced with tunnels and snowsheds—wooden (and now concrete) barriers that protect the tracks in areas prone to high drifting.

To cope with poor weather and visibility on its steep routes, SP developed its famous "Cab-Forward"-type of articulated steam locomotive. As the name implies, these oil-burning locomotives had their cabs at the front of, rather than behind, the boiler, which helped keep the cabs free of smoke during the locomotives' slow grind through tunnels and snowsheds. SP had nearly 200 Cab-Forwards, built between 1928 and 1944. On some SP refrigerator trains, a Cab-Forward would be positioned every 30 cars behind the lead locomotive, serving as

"helpers" to lift the trains over the mountain.

By the end of 1957, SP was fully dieselized. The mountain-climbing sections of the railroad still require helper and "pusher" locomotives to assist moving freights up the steep grades of Donner Pass, Oregon's Cascade Summit, the Tehachapi line in Southern California and other locations.

As outlined earlier, SP comprised numerous subsidiary railroads. Most were of the "paper" variety created for tax or other legal purposes, but a few had identities that, throughout much of their existence, remained at least marginally separate from parent SP. In most cases, these subsidiaries provided important additional feeder traffic, and a few are worth mentioning here. First and foremost was (and is) the St. Louis Southwestern Railway, popularly known as the "Cotton Belt." When SP took control of the SSW in 1932, it was a 1500-mile carrier linking St. Louis and Mem-

ABOVE: The biggest obstacle to smooth traffic flow on the Overland Route—indeed, anywhere on the SP—is "The Hill", better known as Donner Pass, the "Mother of Western Grades." Named for a group of emigrating pioneers that became stranded in the Sierra Range, Donner is a vortex for snow—up to 200 inches during the course of a year. Keeping the route open is a major challenge, one that is met with both permanent structurework (snowsheds over mainline tracks) and mobile devices (rotary snowplows and flangers). Two snow-clad sets of locomotives assigned to flanger (snow pushing) and plow service stand at base of The Hill at Truckee, California in 1993.—BRIAN SOLOMON.

ABOVE: It's the morning of September 8, 1957, and the photographer is waiting to board the *Coast Daylight* at San Francisco for a trip to Los Angeles. Joining other passengers milling (and running) about the platforms of Third & Townsend station, he snapped this photo of the *Daylight*'s locomotive set about to couple onto the train. On this day, a triple-unit combination of Alco and Electro-Motive diesels are assigned to the famous Coast Line speedster.—JOHN DZIOBKO. LEFT: Fast-forward 16 years for this view of Third & Townsend looking northward. The *Coast Daylight* departed from here for the last time in 1971. Now Third & Townsend is strictly a suburban station for San Francisco-San Jose commute trains, one of which is departing behind a Fairbanks-Morse "Train Master" diesel.—TOM POST.

phis with Fort Worth, Dallas and Corsicana, Texas (on SP's Dallas-Houston main line). The Cotton Belt was a perfect way for SP to reach Memphis and St. Louis.

Another notable SP subsidiary was the Northwestern Pacific, stretching some 284 miles north from Sausalito, across from San Francisco, through redwood country to Eureka in far Northern California. NWP was a joint effort of SP and Santa Fe created in 1907. AT&SF sold its interest in NWP to SP in 1929, and SP continued to operate a portion of NWP's southern extremities into the 1990's, although most of the railroad has been sold.

A third SP subsidiary of note was the Pacific Electric, which at one time was the largest electric interurban system in the U.S. PE trackage blanketed metropolitan Los Angeles, extending to San Bernardino, Long Beach, Santa Monica, and countless other destinations. PE offered both freight and extensive passenger services, but the latter was sold to a bus operator in 1953 who by 1962 converted all rail operations to the tire variety. SP continued to operate freight service over many PE lines and merged PE into SP in 1965.

As THE 1950s DREW TO A CLOSE, SP—like many other railroads—came to the conclusion that the intercity passenger train was essentially a dead issue. But whereas many other carriers nursed their diminishing passenger-train fleet

along in the name of good will and public relations, SP in the 1960s did an abrupt about-face, making it entirely clear to travelers that it wanted out of the passenger business. Almost overnight, SP aggressively reduced on-board amenities, and elsewhere numerous secondary trains were entirely discontinued. SP was bent on eliminating all passenger trains, even going so far as to offer purchasing vans for San Francisco commuters if they'd stay off the suburban trains! Public outcry and adamant government agencies such as the Interstate Commerce Commission saved a

ABOVE: SP's original route over the Oregon Cascades was via Ashland and Roseburg, but the 1926 opening of the Natron Cutoff greatly diminished the amount of traffic on the original route, which became known as the Siskiyou Line. Local service, such as this train switching a lumber mill near Grants Pass in 1988, remained until SP turned operations over to another operator in 1994.—MIKE SCHAFER. **BELOW:** Long a popular choice for Hollywood stars was SP's flagship between the Bay Area and Los Angeles, the *Lark*, shown arriving Los Angeles Union Passenger Terminal on a morning in 1957.—JOHN DZIOBKO.

The two views on this page are a study in contrasts between the SP freight of yesteryear with that of 1990s. BELOW: The second section of freight No. 915 labors westbound on the Coast Line near King City, California, in January 1951. A four-unit set of Electro-Motive F3-type diesels leading a train of mixed merchandise in conventional boxcars is representative of the mainstream freight train of the postwar years.—WILLIAM D. MIDDLETON. RIGHT: Forty years later, this SP train winding through the West Bottoms of Kansas City, Missouri, illustrates the evolution of freight handling. Now, much merchandise moves in containers handled "stack" style on special articulated railcar sets that have a low center of gravity. Why containers? Sealed containers can be transferred between transportation modes—rail, water and highway—with relative ease and minimum damage.—DAN MUNSON.

core service over principal SP lines until Amtrak was created to assume intercity passenger service in 1971, and the suburban trains were transferred to a local agency a few years later.

With the passenger problem more or less out of the way, SP concentrated on improved freight operations. One major freight improvement was the 1967 opening of the 78-mile Palmdale Cutoff between Palmdale, on SP's winding line between Mojave and L.A. proper, and Colton (San Bernardino). The Palmdale Cutoff allowed SP freights to bypass the congested L.A. Basin. In 1973, SP opened a new yard at West Colton, which became its main Southern California terminal.

SP's freight traffic itself saw a transformation during the 1970s and 1980's as much traffic—particularly perishables—shifted to trucking. To compensate, SP concentrated on what it could do best: moving bulk commodities such as lumber, chemicals and even coal and expanding piggyback and container services—particularly through L.A. ports, which were seeing a tremendous surge in import traffic.

After the 1970s, SP entered another expansion era, the likes of which hadn't been seen since early in the century. As the Rock Island abandoned in 1980, SP picked up the Rock's Tucumcari-Kansas City-St. Louis line through subsidiary Cotton Belt. Then in 1988—following a failed attempt at merger with Santa Fe—the Southern Pacific was purchased by Rio Grande Industries, owner of the Denver & Rio Grande Western Railroad. This effectively extended SP's reach east from Ogden to Denver, Pueblo and (again) Kansas City.

The next logical step for SP was to penetrate America's leading railroad center, Chicago, where in the 1980s the number of originating and terminating rail shipments were more than double that of any other metropolitan area in the U.S. In 1989, SP finally had its coveted Chicago destination through a new subsidiary, SPCSL (for Southern Pacific Chicago St. Louis) Corporation, which purchased the former Chicago & Alton main line between St. Louis and Chicago. An alternative entry to Chicago came shortly after through a trackage-rights agreement with Burlington Northern (now Burlington Northern Santa Fe) between Kansas City and Chicago. In 1995 SP obtained a third Chicago route over the Santa Fe between Hutchinson, Kansas, and Chicago in settlement of its opposition to the BNSF merger.

As the 20th Century drew to a close, SP was on the brink of perhaps its most ambitious (and controversial) expansion plan ever: merger with Union Pacific. The final decision on this merger, which would make UP the world's largest railroad, will likely happen as this book goes to press. Whatever the outcome, Southern Pacific will always remain one of the well-remembered classics of American railroading.

RIGHT: Although SP's Sunset Route is often associated with the flatlands of Arizona, New Mexico, Texas and Louisiana, it does feature a significant grade—Beaumont Hill. From Indio, California, west, the track climbs over Beaumont Pass (also known as San Gorgonio Pass) sandwiched between the San Bernardino and San Jacinto Mountains to reach San Bernardino and the L.A. Basin. On April 5, 1971, a westbound ore train bound for Kaiser Steel in Fontana, California, snakes down the west slope of Beaumont Hill at Redlands, California, with two sets of helper locomotives, one in the middle of the train and one at the end.—JOE MCMILLAN.

Union Pacific

Union Pacific has long been one of the most powerful and highly respected railroads in North America. Those involved with the infant UP may never have guessed such a rise to fame, for railroad's formative years were fraught with misfortune.

More than anything, the onset of the Civil War prompted UP's formation, which was by act of Congress (the Pacific Rail Act) in 1862. For some time, various potential rail routes to the Pacific had been explored, but not until the South seceded from the Union was there any urgency for actual construction, mainly to keep California in the Union. The Pacific Rail Act also called for Central Pacific to begin construction east from Sacramento, California, to meet UP, which would build west from the Missouri River at Omaha. The two railroads started laying track in 1863.

The meeting of UP and CP at Promontory, Utah, on May 10, 1869, remains one of the most well-recognized rail-related events of American history. (No tableau about UP's history seems complete without the obligatory photo of locomotives UP No. 119 and CP's *Jupiter* meeting pilot to pilot amid a sea of humanity, although we'll dispense with it here.) When the final spike—which was iron and not gold as often thought (gold was too soft to pound into a tie, and the six or so gold spikes present were strictly symbolic)—was driven home at 12:47 p.m. that day, a special telegraphic transmission tripped fire bells in Chicago and lowered a special magnetic ball above the Capitol dome in Washington, D.C.

The UP route headed almost due west from Omaha, following the Platte River almost to Wyoming. Some 30 miles west of Cheyenne, in classic cowboy country, the railroad crossed the Laramie Range at the low end of the Rockies by way of Evans Pass, now known on the railroad as Sherman Hill; the UP's inauspicious crossing of the Continental

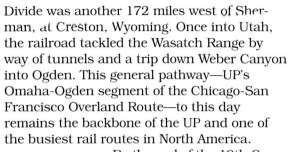

Divide was another 172 miles west of Sherman, at Creston, Wyoming. Once into Utah, the railroad tackled the Wasatch Range by way of tunnels and a trip down Weber Canyon into Ogden. This general pathway—UP's Omaha-Ogden segment of the Chicago-San Francisco Overland Route—to this day remains the backbone of the UP and one of the busiest rail routes in North America.

By the end of the 19th Century, UP had also extended itself into the Pacific Northwest by way of a subsidiary railroad, the Oregon Short Line. This route took off at Granger, Wyoming, just west of Green River, heading northwest through Pocatello and Boise, Idaho, to the Columbia River at Hinkle, Oregon, and followed that waterway to Portland. During this same period, UP's Utah & Northern built from Ogden to Butte, Montana, crossing the OSL at Pocatello. But also by the end of the 1800's, UP had put itself in a precarious position, thanks to mismanagement, heavy debt to the federal government and living and building beyond its means.

The saga of the Union Pacific might have been altogether different in the 20th Century had it not been for one of U.S. railroading's most extraordinary men, Edward H. Harriman, who gained control of UP in 1897. A proponent of heavy investment, Harriman pumped new life into UP and untangled its trail of debt (and some scandal). Like other lines in the Harriman camp, primarily Illinois Central, UP during the ensuing years received a major face lift that included double tracking of the entire main line west of Omaha to Granger, a new, improved route over Sherman Hill, an automatic signaling system, and improved track and right-of-way. Indeed, throughout the first two decades of the 20th Century, UP undertook numerous major line relocations between Cheyenne and Ogden to improve curvature and grades. In many places, the original 1860's-era right-of-way can still be seen from

FACING PAGE: Union Pacific has always done everything in a big way, and this scene at Ogden, Utah, in July 1969 clearly illustrates that moving freight on the UP was big business. Locomotive 16 leading one of two freights about to head east from Ogden is an 8500-hp. gas-turbine electric; it is supplemented by no less than five regular Electro-Motive freight diesels. The Herculean gas-turbines had to have their own separate fuel tender, which can be seen directly behind the gas-turbine's two-unit locomotive. What began as a somewhat frail, hastily built line across Nebraska, Wyoming and Utah, the Union Pacific of today is a monument to the great American railroad dream. FACING PAGE INSET: A bas relief emblem of the Overland Route adorns UP's depot at Cozad, Nebraska.—TWO PHOTOS, MIKE SCHAFER. LEFT: A passenger timetable from 1955.

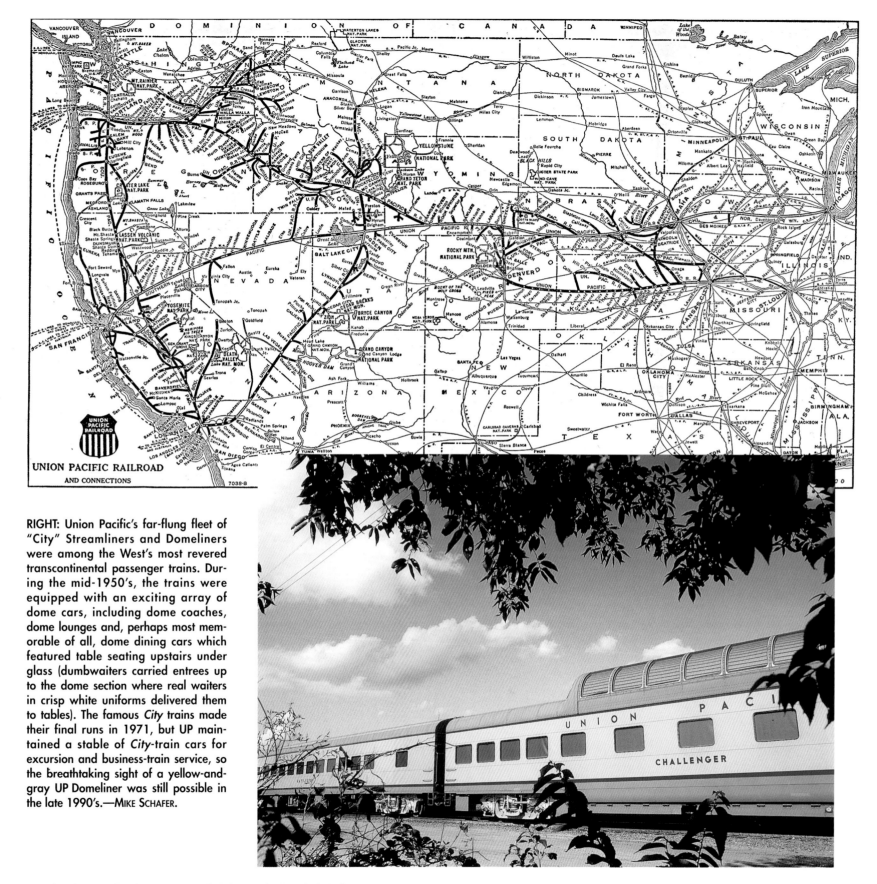

UNION PACIFIC RAILROAD
AND CONNECTIONS

7038-B

RIGHT: Union Pacific's far-flung fleet of "City" Streamliners and Domeliners were among the West's most revered transcontinental passenger trains. During the mid-1950's, the trains were equipped with an exciting array of dome cars, including dome coaches, dome lounges and, perhaps most memorable of all, dome dining cars which featured table seating upstairs under glass (dumbwaiters carried entrees up to the dome section where real waiters in crisp white uniforms delivered them to tables). The famous *City* trains made their final runs in 1971, but UP maintained a stable of *City*-train cars for excursion and business-train service, so the breathtaking sight of a yellow-and-gray UP Domeliner was still possible in the late 1990's.—MIKE SCHAFER.

aboard Amtrak trains that cruise along the Overland Route.

One of the most significant expansions under Harriman was the 1907 opening of UP's Los Angeles & Salt Lake line between Ogden and Los Angeles. Suddenly, UP (allied with Chicago & North Western) became a competitor to be reckoned with in the growing Chicago-Los Angeles market, in terms of both freight and passenger traffic.

When Harriman ran UP, he demanded rolling-stock standardization for economies of scale. Perhaps the most familiar examples were Harriman-style passenger cars, with their distinctive round roofs, that populated the Harriman roads: IC, Southern Pacific and UP.

As locomotive technology advanced, UP management was given to innovation and experimentation. With Harriman's support, superintendent of motive power W. R. McKeen developed an internal-combustion motorcar in 1904 to lower the costs of providing branchline passenger service. UP backed the formation of the McKeen Motor Car Company, which produced 152 "doodlebugs"—as rail motorcars were often called—between 1905 and 1917.

To UP goes the distinction of having sponsored the development of America's first true lightweight streamliner, a three-unit train called the *City of Salina*. Classified by its builder consortium, Pullman-Standard and Electro-Motive Corporation, as the M-10000, the train was unveiled in February 1934. Powered by a distillate engine, the M-10000's high-turret cab and aerodynamic styling captured the imagination of both the public and railroad managements. UP went on to order seven more similar locomotive sets, but equipped with diesel engines, putting them to work on premier transcontinental trains.

It's altogether fitting that UP introduced America's first streamliner, for by mid-century the railroad would boast one of the most highly regarded passenger-train fleets in the country. The little *City of Salina* was a modest somewhere-to-nowhere endeavor, running the 187 miles between Kansas City and Salina, Kansas, but it spawned a whole family of "City" trains that became a transportation institution. A few months after the M-10000 was built in 1934, UP took delivery of its first diesel streamliner, the *City of Portland*, which entered revenue service between Chicago and Portland. In 1936 this was followed by the introduction of the streamliners *City of Los Angeles*, *City of San Francisco*, and *City of Denver*, all three of which were operated in

UNION PACIFIC AT A GLANCE

Headquarters: Omaha, Nebraska

Mileage
- 1950: 9,720
- 1996: 22,785 (includes trackage rights)

Locomotive fleet as of 1963:
- Steam: 29   Diesel: 1,347   Gas-turbine: 49

Rolling-stock fleet as of 1963:
- Freight cars: 54,959   Passenger cars: 851

Principal lines as of 1950:
- Omaha-Ogden, Utah, via Cheyenne, Wyo.
- Ogden-Los Angeles via Las Vegas, Nev.
- Julesburg-La Salle, Colo.
- Granger, Wyo.-Seattle, Wash., via Montpelier, Idaho, and Portland, Oregon
- Pocatello, Idaho-Butte, Mont.
- Hinkle, Ore.-Spokane, Wash.
- Ogden-McCammon (Pocatello)
- Cheyenne/Borie-Kansas City via Denver
- Topeka, Kan.-Gibbon, Neb.
- Marysville, Kan.-Valley (Fremont), Neb.

Principal additional lines added as of 1996:
- Salt Lake City, Utah-Oakland, Calif., via Sacramento, Calif.
- Fremont/Omaha-Chicago
- Nelson, Ill.-St. Louis
- Chicago-Green Bay via Kenosha and Oshkosh, Wis.
- Chicago-Milwaukee via Bain, Wis.
- Milwaukee-Minneapolis
- Minneapolis-Kansas City via Des Moines, Iowa
- Minneapolis-Omaha via Sioux City, Iowa
- Chicago-Madison, Wis.
- Plus the lines of subsidiary Missouri Pacific Lines including:
- Omaha-St. Louis via Kansas City
- Chicago-Houston via Pana, Dupo (St. Louis) and Thebes, Ill., Little Rock, Ark., and Palestine, Texas
- Houston-Brownsville, Texas
- Palestine-Laredo, Texas, via Austin
- Houston-New Orleans via Baton Rouge, La.
- Kansas City-Little Rock, Ark., via Coffeyville, Kan.
- El Paso, Texas-New Orleans via Fort Worth and Shreveport, La.
- Kansas City-Pueblo, Colo.

Notable passenger trains (listed alphabetically:
- *Butte Special* (Salt Lake City, Utah-Butte, Mont.)
- *Challenger* (Chicago-Los Angeles) City of Las Vegas (Los Angeles-Las Vegas)
- *City of Denver* (Chicago-Denver)
- *City of Los Angeles* (Chicago-Los Angeles via Cheyenne, Wyo.)
- *City of Portland* (Chicago-Portland, Ore., via Cheyenne [via Denver 1959-1968])
- *City of Salina* (Kansas City-Topeka-Salina, Kan.)
- *City of St. Louis* (St. Louis-Los Angeles/San Francisco/Portland via Kansas City and Denver)
- *City of San Francisco* (Chicago-Oakland, Calif., via Cheyenne)
- *Columbine* (Omaha-Denver)
- *Forty-Niner* (Chicago-Oakland)
- *Gold Coast* (Chicago-Oakland/Los Angeles)
- *Idahoan* (Cheyenne-Portland via Pocatello)
- *Los Angeles Limited* (Chicago-Los Angeles)
- *Pony Express* (Kansas City-Los Angeles)
- *Portland Rose* (Denver-Portland)
- *San Francisco Overland* (Chicago-Oakland; St. Louis-Oakland after 1955)
- The *Spokane* (Spokane, Wash.-Portland)
- *Utahn* (Cheyenne-Los Angeles)
- *Yellowstone Special* (Pocatello, Idaho-West Yellowstone, Mont.)
- Notes: All UP trains serving Chicago operated Omaha-Chicago via Chicago & North Western until October 1955, then via Milwaukee Road 1955-1971. All UP trains serving St. Louis operated via Wabash between Kansas City and St. Louis.

ABOVE: During the Age of Steam, UP played second to none in harboring massive steam power. Its 4-8-8-4 "Big Boys" were the largest steam locomotives in the world, and not far behind were its 4-6-6-4 "Challenger" types, one of which gingerly steps (if that's possible for a Challenger to do) off the turntable at Cheyenne, Wyoming, in September 1957. RIGHT: Local train No. 27 tromps west from Cheyenne on the morning of September 5, 1957, behind 4-8-4 No. 843. The Northern is equipped with smoke deflectors (also referred to as "elephant ears") to keep smoke moving upward from the locomotive while laboring up grades. Visible in the distance is the spire of UP's Cheyenne depot, then the tallest building in the State of Wyoming.—TWO PHOTOS, JOHN DZIOBKO.

conjunction with C&NW, which relayed the trains between Chicago and Omaha.

The new *City* fleet proved immensely popular, and UP soon found it necessary to upgrade or otherwise re-equip and expand the existing trains to meet demands during the ensuing years. By about 1950, all of the *City* fleet as well as the *San Francisco Overland* had been largely upgraded with newer lightweight streamlined cars. In 1946 UP had added the *City of St. Louis* to the fleet; in 1954 it reintroduced the *Challenger,* and in 1956 it introduced the *City of Las Vegas.*

In 1955, the *City* fleet took on whole new dimension with the addition of "Astra Dome" coaches, lounges, and diners. This move was late in coming for UP, as rival Burlington-Rio Grande-Western Pacific had already introduced dome cars in 1949 on its *California Zephyr,* and Santa Fe had added domes to its transcons in 1950 and 1954.

UP Domeliners were often the trains of choice for stars. Union Pacific played prominently in one of the most-well-remembered "I Love Lucy" episodes, when Lucy and Ricky Ricardo and the Mertzes returned from Hollywood to New York aboard the *City of Los Angeles* (never mind that in reality the train only ran as far east as Chicago). "We're taking the *City of Los Angeles* home!" Lucy cries with excitement. "So that's what's in your suitcase," Ricky retorts as he tries to lift her bag.

Even in the dog days of the American passenger train—the 1960's—UP's passenger trains fared well, relatively speaking. Amtrak assumed most intercity passenger-train operations in 1971, and today vestiges of UP's *City* train fleet survive between Denver and Portland and Salt Lake City and Los Angeles.

In a gratifying twist, however, the *City* Streamliner—in the great tradition of Union Pacific complete with dazzling yellow and gray colors and dome cars—was reborn in the 1980's as the railroad beefed up its business/excursion train program. UP pulled together the remnants of its *City* Streamliner fleet that hadn't been sold to Amtrak or other roads, revamped the cars and even a set of EMD E-series passenger locomotives, and in a blaze of marketing panache dispatched the born-again streamliner to all parts of the expanding UP system to carry excursionists and industry customers alike.

RIGHT: UP pioneered the streamliner, introducing America's first true lightweight streamlined train, the *City of Salina,* in 1934. The Jules Vern-esque train, shown at its birthplace, the Pullman-Standard plant near Chicago, was powered by a distillate engine. Note the horns behind the nose grilles. BELOW: UP also was an early experimenter with motorcar trains such as this putt-putting along the Nebraska countryside.—BOTH PHOTOS, COLLECTION OF MIKE SCHAFER.

FOR MANY YEARS, the Union Pacific has maintained its competitive edge in the arena of freight transport by running long freight trains over rugged terrain for long distances at high speeds. This philosophy required plenty of horsepower up front. During the steam era, UP developed the three-cylinder 4-12-2, the articulated 4-6-6-4 "Challenger", and the 4-8-8-4 "Big Boy"—by most measures the largest steam locomotive ever built. UP partnered with General Electric to apply gas turbine technology to rail transportation, taking delivery of 61 massive gas-turbine locomotives during 1949-1959. Complete dieselization occurred rather late on UP (1959), mostly due to its maintaining an impressive stable of modern steam

power and having ready access to on-line coal mines.

Variety marked the UP diesel fleet, as UP sampled wares from many builders. Never afraid to experiment, UP tinkered with some of its diesels; e.g., adding turbochargers to Electro-Motive GP9 road-switcher diesels to boost horsepower. Emboldened by the UP experiment, EMD went on to apply turbochargers to its standard two-stroke diesel engine in the early 1960's, ushering in what became known as "second generation" diesel locomotives.

During the 1950's, UP superintendent of motive power David Neuhart observed that yearly maintenance costs for most diesels were about the same, be it a 1000-hp. yard switcher or a 1750-hp. mainline locomotive. He commissioned the three major U.S. locomotive builders of that time (General Motors' EMD, American Locomotive Company [Alco] and General Electric) to build twin-engine 5000-5500-hp. locomotives. The theory was that if each of these "beasts" could replace four standard road diesels, a 75 percent maintenance cost saving could be realized. This development resulted in six mammoth locomotive models from the three builders, culminating in EMD's 6600-hp. DD40AX "Centennial" locomotives of 1969, the largest diesel-electrics ever built. The huge DD's performed well, although none of the mega-diesels fully realized the anticipated savings, and no more were built.

The maintenance savings Neuhart envisioned would be accomplished by a concurrent development, the modularization of locomotive components, pioneered by EMD and offered in its "Dash Two" diesel series, marking the third generation of diesel locomotives. The idea was to organize electrical components into modules. Problems could be isolated, the offending module replaced, and the locomotive sent on its way while the module was troubleshooted on the workbench. Like many railroads, UP totally embraced this concept and bought hundreds of EMD SD40-2 and GE C30-7 road diesels, retiring the great variety of motive power rail enthusiasts had come to enjoy. In a way, UP motive-power policy had come full cir-

LEFT: Three EMD locomotives hustle piggyback trailers along UP's 36-mile line connecting Ogden and Salt Lake City on May 22, 1993.—D. B. HARROP.

ABOVE: Not yet within the shroud of L.A. smog, the westbound combined *City of Los Angeles, Challenger,* and *City of Kansas City* wind a serpentine line through California's famous Cajon Pass on November 27, 1970, while overtaking a freight.—JOE MCMILLAN.
RIGHT: UP's coach-only *Challenger* streamliner catered to the economy minded. The train was discontinued in 1947, only to be reintroduced on January 10, 1954. On that day, the first eastbound *Challenger* cruises through Cajon. From 1956 on it was combined with the *City of Los Angeles* during the off season.—WILLIAM D. MIDDLETON.

Always thinking big, Union Pacific experimented with extra-high-horsepower diesel power in the 1960's and 1970's. Working with the three main diesel builders of the time (Electro-Motive, Alco and General Electric), UP wound up with some mammoth motive power. ABOVE: GE's behemoth of this program was its U50C-model diesel, which contained two engines developing a combined 5,000 hp. At Overton, Nebraska, in April 1971, an eastbound freight is in the charge of a smoky U50C and two more-conventional freight diesels, one each from builders Electro-Motive and Alco.—MIKE SCHAFER. Electro-Motive's entry in the develop-double-engine-diesels-for-UP program was the 6,600-hp. DDA40X—dubbed "Centennials" because they were introduced in 1969, the centennial year of the completion of America's first transcontinental railroad. This view of a Centennial at speed coupled to a regular EMD SD40 diesel near Sidney, Nebraska, in 1985 graphically illustrates the impressive girth of the DDA40X.—DAN MUNSON.

cle, reemploying a standardization E. H. Harriman would have approved.

Although UP technically had dieselized by the end of the 1950's, the railroad retained a small stable of serviceable steam locomotives. Notable among these was Northern (4-8-4) No. 844—for a time numbered 8444—which since the "end" of steam on UP has operated on numerous excursion trains as well as on the last westbound *City of Los Angeles* out of Cheyenne on May 1, 1971. The growth in the popularity of UP's steam program prompted the railroad to revive one of its stored articulated "Challenger"-type (4-6-6-4) locomotives, the 3958, in the 1980's.

Union Pacific was active on the merger front. To extend its reach to eastern connections at Chicago and St. Louis (and to thwart competitive proposals), the Union Pacific proposed to merge with the Rock Island in 1964. The regulatory process before the Interstate Commerce Commission dragged on for ten years before conditional approval was granted. By that time, the Rock Island had deteriorated so badly, both physically and financially, that UP was forced to withdraw its merger offer.

In other pursuits for partners, UP was far more successful. In 1982, UP merged with the Western Pacific, giving it the access to Northern California it had previously secured from Southern Pacific. At the same time, UP acquired Missouri Pacific as a subsidiary, reaching Chicago, St. Louis and Texas. In mid-1988, UP absorbed the marginal but pesky Missouri-Kansas-Texas (the "Katy"), if anything to deny it to competitors. In May 1995, Union Pacific took over the Chicago & North Western, its long-time eastern connection. What may be UP's ultimate merger project is pending as this book goes to press. In August 1995, UP and Southern Pacific announced their intention to merge, creating the world's largest railroad.

The consolidation of American railroads is quickly reaching its logical conclusion, which will likely be two or three mega-systems. Chances are that on one of those super railroads, the locomotives will say "Union Pacific" on their flanks.

ABOVE: Summing up UP's prowess in public relations is the slogan billboarded on the side of a caboose trailing a westbound freight near Reno Junction, Nevada, in 1982.—MIKE SCHAFER.

Index